folk art needlecraft

folk art needlecraft

35 step-by-step projects using traditional motifs from across the globe

CLARE YOUNGS

CICO BOOKS

LONDON NEW YORK

Published in 2013 by CICO Books
An imprint of Ryland Peters & Small Ltd
519 Broadway, 5th Floor, New York, NY 10012
20–21 Jockey's Fields, London WC1R 4BW

www.cicobooks.com

10 9 8 7 6 5 4 3 2 1

A CIP catalog record for this book is available from
the Library of Congress and the British Library.

ISBN: 978 1 908862 66 2

Printed in China

Editor: Katie Hardwicke
Designer: Isobel Gillan
Photographer: Caroline Arber
Illustration: Clare and Ian Youngs
Styling: Clare Youngs

For digital editions, visit www.cicobooks.com/apps.php

Contents

Introduction

If asked to characterize a typical piece of folk embroidery you would most likely describe flowers and hearts, with maybe a couple of little birds worked into the design. But the world of folk embroidery and textiles encompasses a multitude of different techniques, motifs, patterns, stitches, and color combinations. I have looked at the different styles across the world, from the brilliantly colored woven textiles of Guatemala and Mexico, the traditional cloth from the African continent, richly worked with symbolic motifs, beautiful and intricate embroideries from across Europe, exotic floral designs from the Far East, appliquéd pattern work from Uzbekistan, to the indigo-dyed and sashiko-stitched garments from Japan and the wonderfully brightly embroidered quilts of India. The variety of stitches, motifs, and patterns across the globe is immense and although many are variations on similar motifs, like stars, triangles, circles, zigzags, flowers, and animals, each country has its distinctive identity. Many contemporary designers and craftsmen are finding inspiration from these ancient and traditional patterns to create pieces for the 21st century that are timeless in their appeal.

Apart from the decorative possibilities, embroidery has its roots in ancient mythology, the spirit world, and religious beliefs. Ancient symbols were worked onto cloth to bring good luck, to protect, to bring prosperity or fertility. Myths and folklore, the surrounding fauna and flora, the animals and birds of each country, have all played a part in the development and characteristics of the many styles that can differ from village to village, from one tribe to another, and region to region. Many of the patterns and motifs stitched today have derived from these ancient symbols handed down through the generations.

I have drawn on these traditions for many of the projects in the book, using embroidery to evoke the wonderful colors and patterns of folk art. The stitches are easy and some of the projects simple for anyone new to stitching. Embroidery is an incredibly relaxing craft and you will be continuing a tradition that has been practised since man first began making clothes!

Today, sewing and the art of embroidery is one of the most popular crafts and more and more people are picking up a needle and thread to start stitching. In an increasingly digital world with everything available at the click of a finger, it is a real pleasure to step back and create something with your own hands. Sewing and embroidery can be a slow process but it is so satisfying to see a design develop from a few drawn lines on a piece of fabric to a finished piece. To place a newly finished cushion on a sofa or see a friend's face light up as they unwrap a hand-embroidered gift is immensely satisfying.

Following the steps in this book you will be able to make beautiful things, too. You need some patience and practise to get a perfect stitch, but I always say that wobbly lines don't matter, it all adds to the folksy charm! You don't need a lot of equipment and you can do the hand-stitched part anywhere—on the train, waiting for the dentist, or on the beach! So, get creative, start stitching, and above all have fun!

Hamsa zipped purse

The hand design, or hamsa, is a universal symbol of protection and is used the world over in all forms of decoration. I based my design on a silver pendant that I have worn for many years. I always take one of these purses when I am traveling, to keep items like small pieces of jewelry safely zipped up inside a suitcase.

Materials

Motifs and stitch guide on page 108

6 × 19 in. (15 × 48 cm) piece of outer fabric, such as cotton or linen

6 × 19 in. (15 × 48 cm) contrasting lining fabric

10¼-in. (26-cm) zipper

Dressmaker's carbon paper

Stranded embroidery floss (cotton) in white and contrasting color

Sewing machine with zipper foot

Matching sewing thread

Scrap of fabric for label

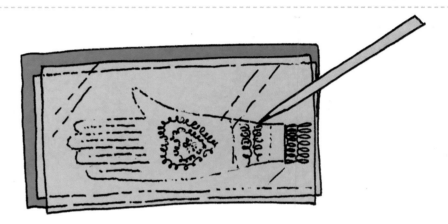

1 Cut the outer and lining fabric in half to make two rectangles, 6 × 9½ in. (15 × 24 cm). Enlarge the hand motif on page 108 by 200 percent and transfer it to one of the rectangles of outer fabric, using dressmaker's carbon paper or a light box. Use the window tracing method if your fabric is pale in color (see page 121). Follow the stitch guide on page 108 to embroider the design with white embroidery floss (cotton).

2 Place one piece of lining fabric on your work surface with the right side facing up. Lay the zipper along the top of the fabric and then place the outer fabric with the embroidered side face down on top, lining up the top edges. Pin all three layers together.

3 Using a zipper foot, machine stitch along the top edge to secure the zipper. Keep your stitching closer to the zipper teeth than the top edge but not so close that the zipper gets stuck.

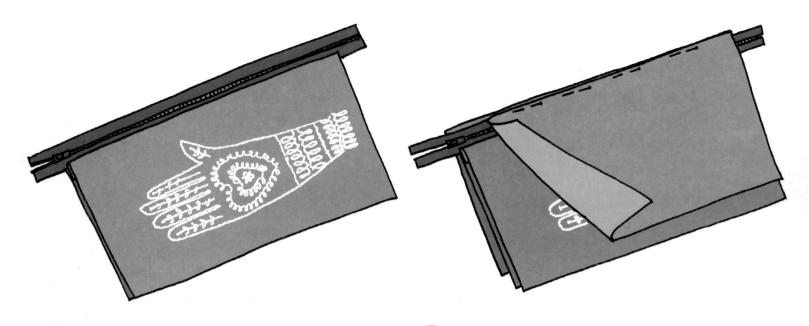

4 Fold back the front and back pieces so that the wrong sides are together—this will reveal the other side of the zipper. Press along the seam.

5 Repeat steps 2 and 3 with the remaining pieces of lining fabric and undecorated outer fabric on this side of the zipper.

Once you have mastered the lined and zipped purse you can make different sizes and adapt some of the embroidered motifs in the book to fit.

6 To make the label, cut a piece of fabric 3¼ × 1¾ in. (8 × 4.5 cm). Fold in half and crease the fabric to mark the middle. Embroider the heart motif on page 108 in a contrasting color or color to match the label, centering the heart between the top and bottom edges and ½ in. (1 cm) in from the middle fold. Fold in half with right sides together. Sew along each edge, trim the seam allowance, turn right side out, and press.

7 Take both pieces of lining to one side, with right sides together, and take both pieces of outer fabric to the other side, again with right sides together. With the outer fabric nearest to you and the wrong side of the embroidery facing up, place the label with the heart facing up sandwiched between the two outer sections of fabric on the left side, 1¼ in. (3 cm) down from the top edge.

8 Open up the zipper halfway and pin all around the edge of the outer and lining sections. Machine stitch all around, taking a ½-in. (1-cm) seam and leaving a 2½-in. (6-cm) gap on the bottom edge of the lining section.

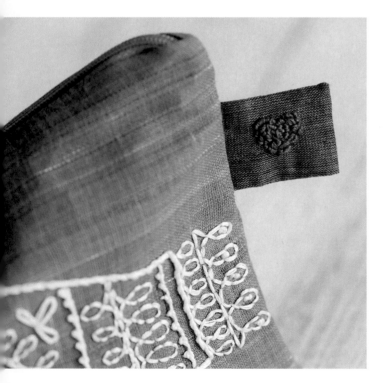

9 Trim the seam allowance and cut across the corners. Slipstitch the gap in the lining closed. Turn the purse the right way out, tucking the lining into the purse, and press.

Travel sewing kit

On a recent trip to Budapest in Hungary, I fell in love with the small felt purses, decorated in traditional felt appliqué designs, which seemed to be on sale in every other store and market stall. They made great gifts and I decided that I could adapt the design to make this useful travel sewing kit.

Materials

Motif and stitch guide on page 108

Approx. 10 × 10 in. (25 × 25 cm) felt in two colors

Pinking shears (optional)

Cream stranded embroidery floss (cotton)

Air-erasable marker pen

Snap fastener

1 For the outer section, cut a piece of felt measuring 10 × 4¾ in. (25 × 12 cm). For the lining, cut a piece of contrasting felt measuring 7 × 5 in. (18 × 13 cm). Use pinking shears, if you have them, to cut out the rectangles and give a pretty decorative edge.

2 Trace the motif for the front section onto tracing paper. It is quite difficult to use dressmaker's carbon paper on fluffy material like felt, so cut out the main shapes from the tracing paper, pin the shapes to the felt, and draw around them with an air-erasable marker. The stitching is quite simple so that you can fill in the outlines by looking at the template and working by eye. Don't worry too much about wobbly lines, it is all part of the folksy charm! Center the design on the height and approx ¼ in. (5 mm) in from the edge.

3 Lay the lining piece of felt on a flat surface. Position the outer piece over the top with right side facing, so that an equal amount of lining felt is visible on either side and along the top decorated edge. Pin in position, placing the pins on the reverse side, as you will be sewing on the other side.

4 Turn the felt over and turn up the bottom section of the outer piece and pin along each edge, making sure that the lining is visible on each side. Machine stitch up one side to the top, along the top, and down the other side.

5 Sew one part of the snap fastener to the inside flap, positioning it in the center and ¾ in. (2 cm) down from the top edge. Sew the other part of the fastener to the bottom inside section, making sure that the two parts match up.

Hedgehog craft bag

The embroidery on this bag is a bit like stitch doodling! It is a great way to practice some basic stitches and do some designing. Follow the template to stitch in the spines and then work along each spine filling the length with triangles, knots, circles, and stars. You can draw out a plan but I think it is much more fun to make it up as you go along.

Materials

Motif and stitch guide on page 108

31½ × 15 in. (80 × 38 cm) piece of fabric, such as heavyweight linen or cotton drill

Dressmaker's carbon paper

Stranded embroidery floss (cotton), in two colors

1.5 yd (1.5 m) webbing, 1½ in. (3.5 cm) wide

10¼ × 4½ in. (27 × 11 cm) piece of felt, plus a scrap for the label

1 Cut the linen or cotton in half to make two rectangles measuring 15¾ × 15 in. (40 × 38 cm) each. Take one of the pieces of fabric and place with the widest measurement at the base. Mark a point 1½ in. (3.5 cm) in from each side edge, along the top. On the left side, draw a line from the lower corner to meet the mark at the top. Repeat on the right side so that you have a shape that is wider at the bottom and slants in at the top. Cut the shape out and repeat for the other piece of fabric.

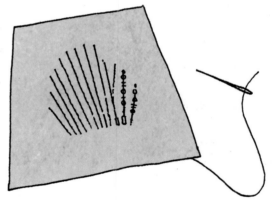

2 Enlarge the motif on page 108 by 200 percent and trace the spines of the hedgehog. Using dressmaker's carbon paper, transfer the design onto the fabric, centering it between the side edges and starting 4½ in. (11 cm) up from the bottom edge.

3 Stitch the spines using whipped backstitch, then you can start stitch doodling, working your way up each spine. To help plan your design, transfer the basic hedgehog shape with the spines onto paper and draw in shapes like triangles, dots, or squares along the spines, looking at the photograph of the finished bag for inspiration. Then simply start stitching—you can make a variety of shapes with just three different stitches.

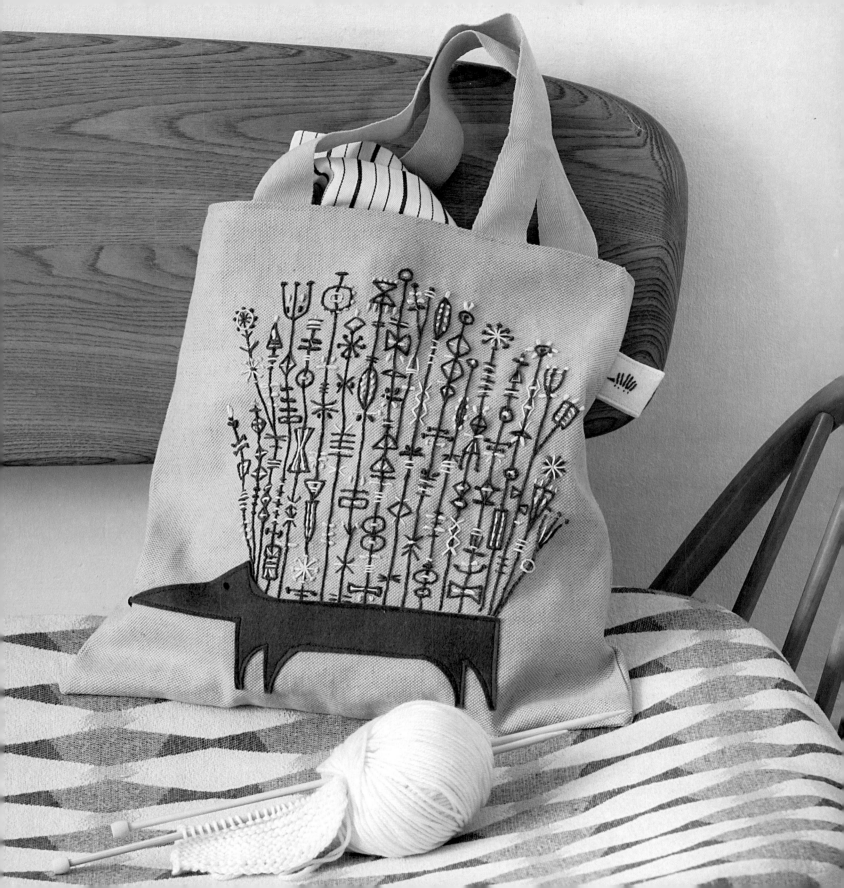

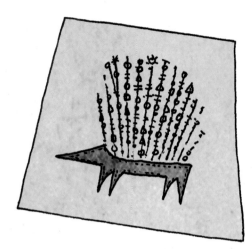
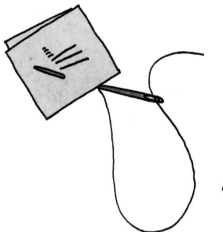
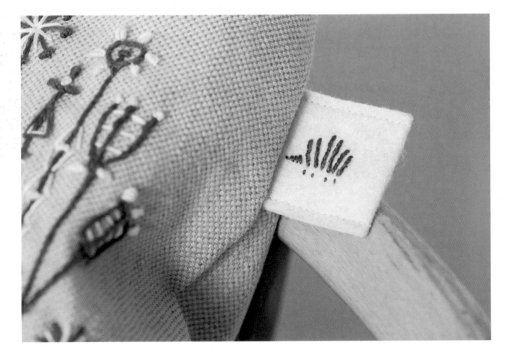

4 Enlarge the body on page 108 by 200 percent and cut out the shape from felt. Pin it in position so that the ends of the spines meet the body. Machine topstitch all around the felt body, close to the edge. Make a bullion knot for the eye and nose.

5 To make the label, cut a piece of felt 3¼ × 1½ in. (8 × 3.5 cm). Fold it in half, making a crease with your finger to mark the middle. Embroider the small hedgehog motif on page 108, centering it between the top and bottom and ½ in. (1 cm) in from the crease. Sew the top and bottom seams, close to the edge.

6 With right sides facing, pin the front and back sections of the bag together. With the wrong side of the embroidered piece facing you, place the label in the seam sandwiched between the front and back with the embroidered side facing up, 2¾ in. (7 cm) down from the top edge, with the raw edges aligned. Machine stitch down each side and across the bottom, taking a ½-in. (1-cm) seam. Trim the seam allowance and cut across the corners. For a neat finish, you could zigzag all the raw edges.

7 Cut three pieces of webbing: one piece 26½ in. (67 cm) and two pieces for the handles, each 19 in. (48 cm) in length. Fold over the top edge of the bag by ½ in. (1 cm) and press.

8 Starting at the side seam, pin the longer length of webbing along the top edge of the bag, lining up the top of the webbing to the top of the folded edge. At the same time, position the ends of the handles sandwiched between the webbing and the bag. Place the two ends 3½ in. (9 cm) in from each side and aligning the ends of the straps with the bottom edge of the webbing lining the top of the bag. Take care that the straps aren't twisted. When you have come full circle, fold over the extra bit of webbing and pin it down over the raw end on the side seam.

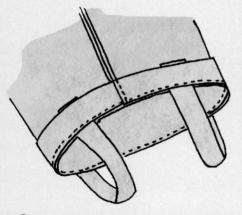

9 Machine stitch all around the top edge, catching the straps in the stitching. Machine stitch the webbing at the side seam where it overlaps. Turn the bag right side out and press.

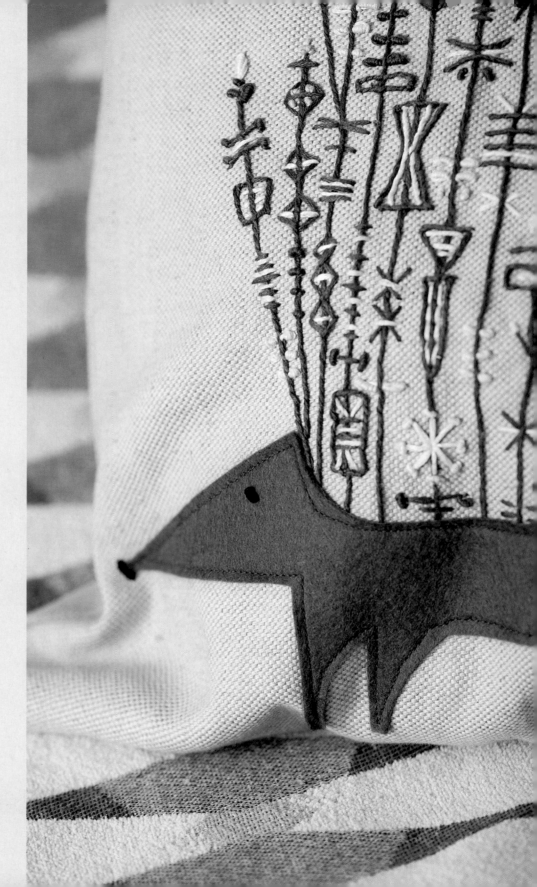

Drawstring bag

The bird image is a popular motif in folk art design. These two delightful birds, entwined amongst flowers and leaves, look lovely stitched onto linen and made into a practical drawstring bag. Try using it as a toy bag or to carry your child's dance kit—you'll wonder how you ever managed without it!

Materials

Motif and stitch guide on page 109

½ yd (½ m) cream linen or cotton drill

Dressmaker's carbon paper

Sewing machine

Matching sewing thread

Stranded embroidery floss (cotton) in indigo, pink, orange, green, and yellow

Air-erasable marker pen

64 in. (1.6 m) cord

Safety pin

Scraps of felt

1 Using the linen or cotton drill, cut out two rectangles measuring 16¼ × 13½ in. (42 × 34 cm). Enlarge the motif on page 109 by 155 percent and, using dressmaker's carbon paper, transfer the motif onto one of the rectangles. Center the design between each side edge and place the base of the design 3¼ in. (8 cm) up from the bottom edge. Follow the stitch guide on page 109 to embroider the design.

2 Pin the front and back of the bag with right sides together. Starting and finishing 5 in. (12.5 cm) from the top edge of each side, taking a ½-in. (1-cm) seam, machine stitch along the bottom edge and the sides.

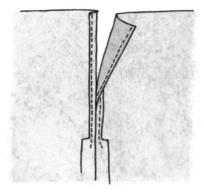

3 Make a ½-in. (1-cm) snip on each raw side edge, just above the seam. On each raw side edge, turn a ¼-in. (5-mm) double hem on both the front and the back of the panels. Pin and machine stitch, continuing the stitching ½ in. (1 cm) into the seam that joins the back and front panels together.

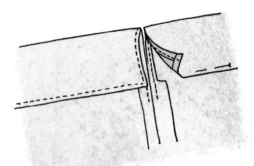

4 Turn under a ½-in. (1-cm) hem to the wrong side along the top edge of both the front and back panels. Press, then turn in a 2½-in. (6-cm) hem, pin in position, and machine stitch close to the edge.

5 Using an air-erasable marker, mark a line ¾ in. (2 cm) above this hem. Machine stitch along this line on both the back and the front of the bag to form a channel.

6 Attach a safety pin to one end of the length of cord and thread the cord through the channel on one side of the bag, then back through the other side. Take the cord around once more on both sides so that you have a double row of cord on each side.

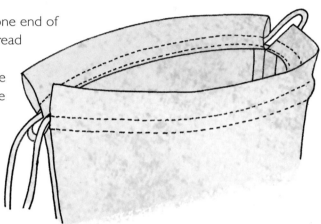

7 Take hold of one piece of cord on each side of the bag and pull to draw the top part of the bag together, making sure the same amount of cord protrudes on each side.

8 Trace the tag template on page 109 and cut out 4 felt tags. Embroider the pattern on two of the tags. With wrong sides together, pin one front and one back tag together over the ends of the cord on each side of the bag. Machine stitch all around the tags, as close to the edge as possible, to attach them to the cord, making sure you catch the cord in the stitching.

9 Trim the seam allowance and snip across the corners. Turn the bag right side out and press.

These two delightful birds, entwined amongst flowers and leaves, look lovely stitched onto linen.

Picnic bag

When I go on a picnic, I like to have an old-fashioned rug, a pretty vintage thermos flask, china cups and plates, and beautiful looking, but simple picnic food. Of course, everything has to be carried in the right kind of bag and this smart and roomy bag in striking red, white, and blue will complete the stylish look. Any stripy fabric, like ticking, will work well.

Materials

Motif and stitch guide on page 109

43 × 20 in. (110 × 50 cm) ticking fabric

40 × 5 in. (100 × 12 cm) ticking fabric, for handles

Tracing paper and pencil

Dressmaker's carbon paper

Red stranded embroidery floss (cotton)

Sewing machine and matching sewing thread

1 Cut the large piece of fabric in half to make two rectangles, 21½ × 20 in. (55 × 50 cm) for the bag. Cut the strip of fabric in half to make two strips, 20 × 5 in. (50 × 12 cm) for the handles. Enlarge the design on page 109 by 155 percent and transfer it on to one of the rectangles of fabric. Position a motif at each side, 1¾ in. (4 cm) in from the side edge and 5½ in. (14 cm) up from the bottom edge. Repeat the motif a third time, centering it between the two on either side.

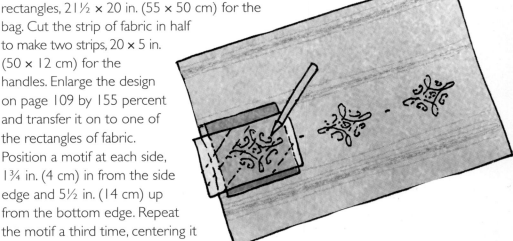

2 Follow the stitch guide on page 109 to embroider the design in bullion knots. Place a bullion knot either side of the central motif, centered between the motifs at the side.

3 With right sides facing, place the back and front sections together aligning the raw edges. Pin each side and the bottom edge and machine stitch together, taking a ½-in. (1-cm) seam. Machine stitch a row of zigzag along the raw edges on the three sides.

This smart and roomy bag in striking red, white, and blue will complete any stylish picnic.

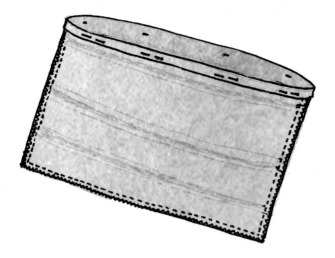

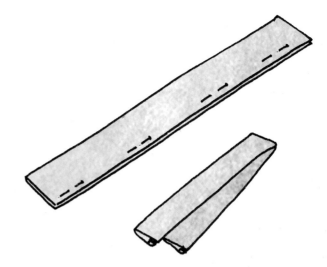

4 Turn over a double ½-in. (1-cm) hem all around the top edge. Pin and machine stitch. Press.

5 With right sides together, fold one of the strips of fabric in half. Pin and stitch a ½-in. (1-cm) seam along the edge. Trim the seam allowance and turn right side out. Press. Repeat with the other strip of fabric.

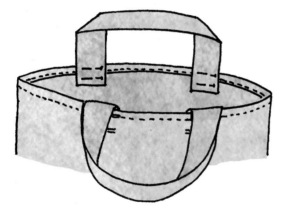

6 Fold in the raw edges by ½ in. (1 cm) at either end of one of the strips. Pin each end to the inside top edge of the bag, positioning the ends 1¾ in. (4 cm) down inside the bag and 5½ in. (14 cm) in from each side. Machine stitch two lines of stitching ½ in. (1 cm) down and 1¼ in. (3 cm) down from the top edge. To strengthen the bag it is best to machine sew the line a few times. Repeat on the other side of the bag with the second handle.

7 With the bag inside out, fold the side seam flat toward the bottom center seam, until the corner of the bag makes a triangle. Stitch across the triangle 2 in. (5 cm) down from the top point of the triangle. Trim off the point to a ½ in. (1 cm) seam allowance and stitch a line of zigzag along the raw edge. Repeat for other side seam. Turn the bag right side out.

Make-up bag

Once you have mastered the technique of a zipped and lined purse, you will be able to make all sorts of useful little bags. This one is the perfect size for a make-up bag. The design is based on traditional Hungarian embroidery but you could use any of the motifs in the book and adapt them to embellish your bag.

Materials

Motifs and stitch guide on page 109

12 × 8 in. (30 × 20 cm) outer fabric

12 × 8 in. (30 × 20 cm) lining fabric

Tracing paper and pencil

Dressmaker's carbon paper

Stranded embroidery floss (cotton) in a bright color

8¾ in. (22 cm) zipper

Sewing machine with zipper foot

Matching sewing thread

1 Cut the outer and lining fabric in half to make two rectangles, 6 × 8 in. (15 × 20 cm). Enlarge the heart motif on page 109 by 135 percent and transfer it to one of the rectangles of outer fabric, using dressmaker's carbon paper or a light box. Use the window tracing method if your fabric is pale in color (see page 121). Follow the stitch guide on page 109 to embroider the design.

2 Place one piece of lining fabric on your work surface with right side facing up. Lay the zipper along the top of the fabric and then place the outer fabric with the embroidered side face down on top, lining up the top edges. Pin all three layers together.

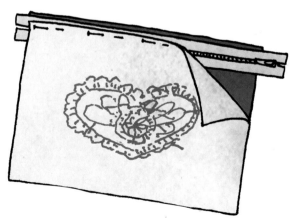

3 Using a zipper foot, machine stitch along the top edge to secure the zipper. Keep your stitching closer to the zipper teeth than the top edge but not so close that the zipper gets stuck.

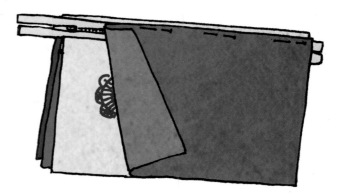

4 Fold back the front and back pieces so that the wrong sides are together—this will reveal the other side of the zipper. Press along the seam.

5 Repeat steps 2 and 3 with the remaining pieces of lining fabric and undecorated outer fabric on this side of the zipper.

6 Bring both sides of the lining to one side and take both pieces of outer fabric to the other side. Open the zipper halfway and pin all around the edge of the outer and lining sections. Machine stitch all around, taking a ½-in. (1-cm) seam and leaving a 2½-in. (6-cm) gap on the bottom edge of the lining section.

7 Trim the seam allowances and cut across the corners. Turn the purse right sides out, slipstitch the gap in the lining closed, then tuck the lining into the purse. Press.

The design is based on
traditional Hungarian
embroidery.

Bird and beastie softies

Many of the patterns and motifs in embroidery hold great significance and meaning, having evolved through centuries of hunting rituals, customs, folklore, and mythology. These beasties were inspired by the wonderfully strange shaped creatures that are worked into the beautiful kantha embroidered quilts of India and Bangladesh.

Materials

Motifs and stitch guides on page 110

Approx. 8 × 12 in. (20 × 30 cm) piece of felt for each beastie

Dressmaker's carbon paper (optional)

Air-erasable marker pen

Stranded embroidery floss (cotton) in contrasting color

Scraps of felt or fabric for labels

Fiberfill (polyester) toy stuffing

1 Trace the animal motifs on page 110 and cut out the shapes from felt. You can use dressmaker's carbon paper to transfer the design to be stitched onto the shapes or, as the design is quite simple, you could draw directly onto the felt with an air-erasable marker.

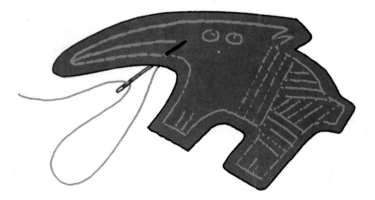

2 Follow the stitch guide on page 110 to embroider the design. It is all stitched in whipped backstitch and bullion knots—very easy!

3 For the label, cut out a piece of fabric measuring 2¾ × 1½ in. (7 × 3.5 cm). Fold the fabric in half and crease to mark the middle. Draw the design on page 110 onto the label with an air-erasable marker, centering it between the top and bottom edges and ⅛ in. (3 mm) in from the marked crease. Embroider the design then fold the fabric in half, with right sides together, and sew the top and bottom edges. Trim the seam allowance, turn right side out, and press.

4 With wrong sides together, pin the back and front of the beastie together, sandwiching the label in between the two pieces of fabric along the back seam, with the raw edges aligned. Machine stitch around the shape, close to the edge, leaving a 2-in. (5-cm) gap along one of the seams.

5 Push small amounts of fiberfill (polyester) stuffing through the gap and into the small outer parts, such as the feet and tail, first. Use the end of a small paintbrush to help push the stuffing into the spaces. Continue stuffing until the shape is firm and then hand stitch the gap closed using a small backstitch.

Floral booties

Floral motifs are one of the most popular decorative embellishments, from richly textured Chinese silk embroideries to the geometric, stylized floral patterns on linen aprons in Eastern Europe. These little shoes are made from linen and lined with pretty fabric. I have used simple bullion knots to form the charming, raised flower design.

Materials

Templates, motifs, and stitch guide on page 111

Approx. 12 × 12 in. (30 × 30 cm) outer fabric, such as linen

Approx. 12 × 12 in. (30 × 30 cm) lining fabric, such as printed cotton

Blue and red stranded embroidery floss (cotton)

1 Enlarge the templates and motifs on page 111 by 135 percent and cut out the shapes for the upper and sole from the outer and lining fabrics. Follow the stitch guide on page 111 to embroider the flowers onto the outer section of the shoe. Sew the line of stitching around the top edge of the shoe, ⅝ in. (1.5 cm) down from the top. If you lay your pieces with the top edge facing you, position the flowers on the right side for the right shoe and on the opposite side for the left shoe.

2 For the right shoe, take the outer piece and lining and place them right sides together. Pin and machine stitch along the top edge taking a ½-in. (1-cm) seam. Trim the seam allowance, turn right side out, and press.

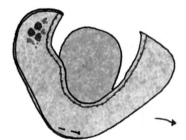

3 Mark the center point along the bottom edge of the upper piece and the center point of the sole lining. Lay the sole lining, right side facing up, on a flat surface. Pin the upper and sole together, aligning the center points. Continue to pin the rest of the upper to the sole lining, easing the fabric around the curve and making sure that the side with the embroidery overlaps the plain side. Machine stitch around the heel section and baste (tack) the rest of the upper around the edge.

4 Position the outer sole piece over the top of the upper section. Pin and baste (tack) in place to just beyond the machine-stitched section at the heel. Machine stitch this section. Remove the basting stitches and trim the seam allowance.

5 Turn the shoe right side out. Fold over the unstitched raw edge of the sole, to match the seam already sewn. Tuck in the raw edges of the top section and slipstitch all around the back of the heel to close the gap.

6 Repeat for the left shoe, remembering to overlap the opposite way so that the embroidery is on the top.

Inca hat

Keep your baby snug and stylish in this Peruvian inspired hat. Ancient symbols and motifs that have been passed on through the generations, like this little bird, are still used today and adorn handmade colorful bags, hats, and blankets, traditionally made from soft, warm alpaca wool and colored with natural plant dyes.

Materials

Template, motif, and stitch guide on page 111

12½ × 7 in. (32 × 18 cm) gray felted wool—mine was made from an old woolen sweater machine washed on the hottest setting

Stranded embroidery floss (cotton) in white, turquoise, and brown

Small amount of blue yarn

Air-erasable marker pen

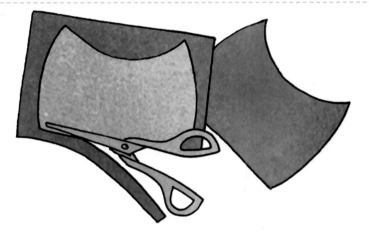

1 Enlarge the template for the hat on page 111 by 200 percent. Cut out a front and back piece from the felted wool.

2 Trace and cut out the shape for the bird from the motif on page 111. Pin it to the front piece, positioning it ½ in. (1 cm) up from the bottom edge in the center. Draw around the shape with an air-erasable marker.

3 Follow the stitch guide on page 111 to embroider the design for the bird. Pin the front and back pieces with right sides together and machine stitch the sides and top, taking a ½-in. (1-cm) seam. Trim the seam allowance and turn right side out. Use the end of a thin paintbrush to push up into the corners.

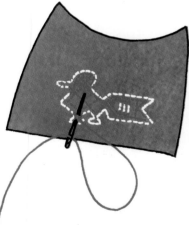

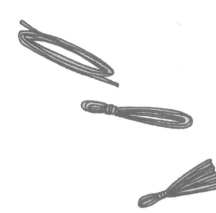

4 To make the tassels, wind some yarn around three fingers a few times. Slip the yarn from your fingers and wind a shorter length of yarn around one end. Tie with a knot to secure. Trim the loops at the opposite end to make a tassel approximately 1½ in. (3.5 cm) long. Repeat to make a second tassel.

5 Hand stitch a tassel to each corner tip to complete the hat.

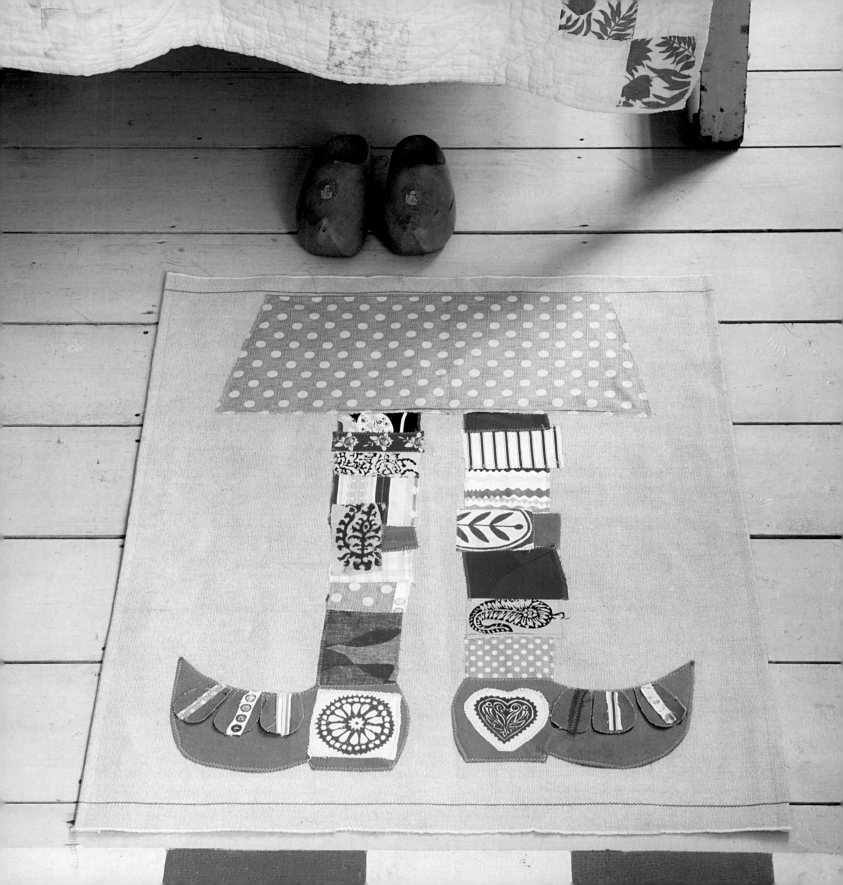

Pippi rug

One of my favorite books as a child was *Pippi Longstocking* by the Swedish author, Astrid Lindgren. Pippi was a nine-year-old girl who lived on her own with a monkey and a horse, possessed superhuman strength, had wild adventures with two neighboring children—and wore stripy socks!

Materials

Template on page 111

Two × 8 × 5 in. (20 × 12 cm) pieces solid (plain) fabric or felt for the clogs

Scraps of brightly colored fabric for the petals and stripy stockings

15 × 6¾ in. (38 × 17 cm) patterned fabric for the skirt

27½ × 21½ in. (70 × 55 cm) heavyweight cotton or canvas for the rug

Air-erasable marker pen

Sewing machine

Matching sewing thread

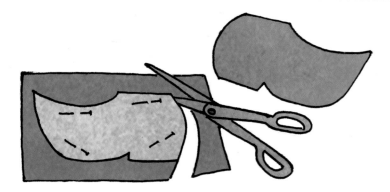

1 Enlarge the template for the clog and petal-shaped decoration on page 111 by 200 percent. Pin the clog shape to the right side of one piece of solid fabric. Draw around the shape and cut it out. Turn the template over and pin it to the right side of the second piece of fabric and repeat. Use the petal-shaped template to cut out 6 shapes from the scraps of fabric.

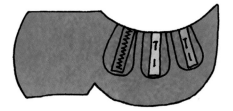

2 Take the fabric for the skirt, and use an air-erasable marker to mark 2 in. (5 cm) in from each side on the long top edge. Using a ruler, draw a line from the bottom right-hand corner to join up with the mark along the right top edge. Repeat on the left-hand side. Cut along these two lines to make a trapezoid shape for the skirt.

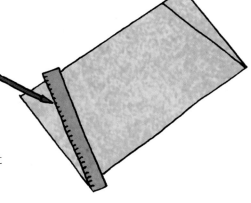

3 Cut out six strips of fabric to fit the length of the petal shapes. Position three petal shapes along the front of the clog, lining up the flat end of the petal with the top edge of the clog. Pin a strip in position in the center of each shape and secure with a line of machine zigzag.

4 Cut out a piece of fabric to decorate the heel end of the clog. You could cut a shape, such as a heart, or cut a motif from patterned fabric. Pin in position on the heel and machine zigzag to secure.

5 Pin the clogs to the rug fabric, placing them approx. 1½ in. (3.5 cm) apart and 3¼ in. (8 cm) up from the bottom edge. Pin the skirt to the top of the rug, centered on the width and ¾ in. (2 cm) down from the top edge. Sew a line of zigzag all around the edge of the skirt to secure it in place.

6 With an air-erasable marker, draw two lines up from the top of the clog to the base of the skirt to make a leg. Repeat from the other clog.

7 Cut out pieces of fabric in different-sized rectangles and squares and position them along the leg shapes. You can overlap the pieces and go over the marked lines—you want to achieve a jumbled, haphazard look and a good mix of colors.

8 When you are happy with the arrangement, pin the pieces in place and machine zigzag all around the edges.

9 Turn under a double ½-in. (1-cm) hem all around the sides of the rug, pin, and machine stitch. You may find that the fabric is too thick to sew a double hem. If it is, sew a line of zigzag all around the edge, turn under a ¾-in. (2-cm) single hem, and sew a line of stitching ½ in. (1 cm) in on all sides. Press.

I have tried to find the brightest scraps of fabric possible to depict Pippi's colorful character.

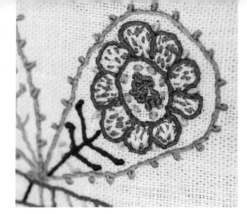

Framed butterfly

Small embroideries are ideal for framing. This brightly colored design would look lovely in a child's bedroom. You could make it as a special gift for a new baby or a first birthday.

Materials

Motif and stitch guide on page 112

Piece of linen or suitable fabric

Air-erasable marker pen

Stranded embroidery floss (cotton) in different colors

Frame

Fabric glue or masking tape

1 I have used an 11 in. (28 cm) square frame. It has a 9 in. (23 cm) square opening, so I have cut a square piece of fabric to cover the backing board, allowing an extra ¾ in. (2 cm) all around to overlap. You may have to adjust the size of your fabric to fit your frame. I removed the glass.

2 Enlarge the motif on page 112 by 155 percent. If the embroidery is to be sewn onto a pale piece of fabric you can use a light box or window tracing method to transfer the design onto the fabric (see page 121).

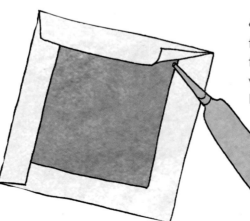

3 Follow the stitch guide on page 112 to embroider the design. Use any colors you like—I chose a selection of my brightest colored threads.

4 Take out the backing board for the frame. Place the embroidered fabric flat on your work surface with the wrong side facing up. Place the backing board over the top, leaving an equal border of fabric all around. Fold the overlapping edges down and secure with fabric glue or masking tape, before replacing the board in the frame.

Daisy dress

The fresh appearance of a gingham summer dress never loses its appeal. The pretty rows of embroidery all add to the simple charm. With tie straps, this is easily adjusted to fit. Using the squares of gingham as a guide for your stitching, it couldn't be simpler!

Materials

To fit ages 5–7 years; simply adjust the length to fit younger or older children

Motif and stitch guide on page 112

Approx. 1 yd (1 m) gingham fabric

Air-erasable marker pen

Long ruler

Stranded embroidery floss (cotton) in dark pink, pale pink, pale blue, green, light green, and yellow

Sewing machine and matching sewing thread

1 From the fabric, cut two rectangles 23½ × 22 in. (60 × 56 cm) and one strip 43¼ × 1½ in. (110 × 3.5 cm). Along the top, short edge of one of the rectangles, make a mark 2½ in. (6 cm) in from each side. Draw a line from this mark down to the bottom corner, on each side. If you don't have a long ruler you could use a sheet of newspaper or fold the fabric and crease with your fingernail to mark the line. Cut off the marked triangle at each side. Repeat with the other piece of fabric.

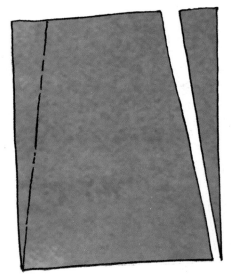

2 Follow the stitch guide on page 112 to embroider the patterns. Sew the daisies, starting 2¾ in. (7 cm) down from the top edge and placing them in a random arrangement on the top section of the dress. Start the first row of stitching 2¾ in. (7 cm) up from the bottom.

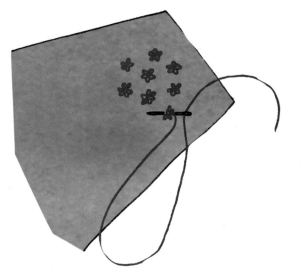

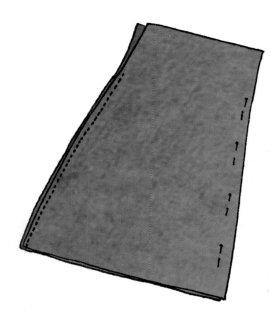

3 With right sides facing, pin the back and front sections together. Machine stitch a ½-in. (1-cm) seam along each side edge, stopping 6 in. (15 cm) from the top.

4 Along one of the open seams, fold over a double ¼ in. (5 mm) seam. Pin and machine stitch. Repeat on the adjacent side to make the lower part of the armhole. Repeat on the other side of the dress. Sew a line of zigzag stitching along the raw edges of the seam, running down from the bottom of the armhole to the lower edge of the dress on each side.

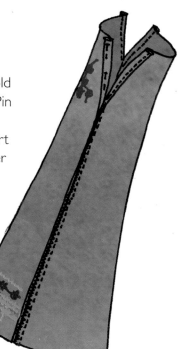

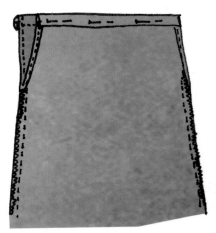

5 Along the top edge of the front section, fold over ¼ in. (5 mm) and then fold again by ⅜ in. (1.5 cm) to make a channel to thread the tie through. Pin and machine stitch close to the edge of the fold. Repeat on the back of the dress.

6 To make the tie, take the long strip of fabric, fold it in half with wrong sides facing, and fold in the raw edges by ¼ in. (5 mm) along its length. Pin together, folding in the raw edges at each end by ½ in. (1 cm). Machine stitch along the length and across each end of the tie.

7 Attach a safety pin to one end of the tie. Starting at the right side of the front panel, feed the strap into the channel at the top of the dress and out on the left side. Feed the tie through the back channel, leaving a loop to form a strap, and out on the right side.

8 Tie off the ends of the strap on the right side of the dress in a bow, leaving a loop the same length as the loop on the other armhole. Gather the fabric along the front and back—you may have to do some adjusting to get the straps the right length and even on each side.

9 Turn over a double ½-in. (1-cm) hem on the bottom edge of the dress. Pin, machine stitch, and then press to finish.

Pin dolls

These two enchanting little ladies are based on traditional Guatemalan worry dolls. In folklore, children were told to whisper their worries to tiny pin dolls, place them under their pillow, and the dolls would take their worries away while they slept.

Materials

Templates and stitch guide on page 112

Thin wire

A small pair of pliers

Scraps of felt

Matching sewing thread

Orange and pink stranded embroidery floss (cotton) and small amounts of other colors

Small lengths of ribbon and trimmings

1 Cut three lengths of wire measuring 3½ in. (9 cm). Take the first piece and form it into a loop, twisting the two ends together to secure. Squeeze the loop to make a thinner, elongated shape and twist the loop at about 2 in. (5 cm) down from the top to form the head.

2 Take the second piece of wire and form it into a loop, as in step 1. Squeeze the loop together, fold it in half to find the center, and wrap it once or twice around the neck to form the arms. Repeat for the legs but place the folded piece of wire through the bottom of the body loop. Twist around once to secure and bend the bottom of the wire up a fraction on each end to make the feet.

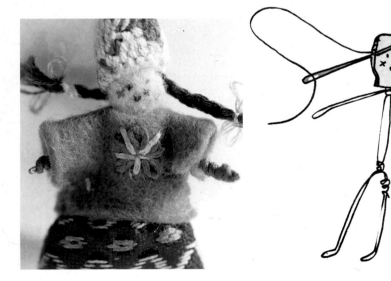

3 Trace the template on page 112 and cut out a piece of felt for the head. On one side sew a tiny dot for each eye, two tiny dots side by side for the mouth, and a small cross stitch for each cheek. As the stitches are so small you will need to use normal, thin sewing thread. Fold the felt in half and position it over the wire head. Sew up the side seams using small stitches.

4 To cover the arms, take a length of pink stranded embroidery floss (cotton) and wind it around the arm, starting at the hand on one side. Lay the end of the thread along the length of the arm to hide it behind the winding thread.

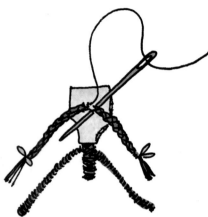

5 Twist the thread around the neck a couple of times and continue down the arm to the hand, come back up the arm, then continue down the body. You can continue down the legs in the same color or change to another color—I used orange. Come back up the legs to tie off at the body section. It is quite tricky to cover up the wire at the tip of the toes. I tied a tiny amount of thread through the wire, tied a knot, and trimmed it. This hides the wire and adds a tiny tassel for a shoe!

6 Use a 2-in. (5-cm) length of embroidery floss to make a braid (plait). Use a contrasting color to tie off the braid at each end, and secure it to the back of the head with a few stitches so that the doll has bunches.

7 Cut a piece of ½-in. (1-cm) wide trimming or ribbon to approx. 1¼ in. (3 cm) long. Cut off two triangles at the corners, one from each side, so that the ribbon is a trapezoid shape. Fold it around to form a cone, tuck under the raw edge with a very small hem and sew together. Place it over the head to make a hat and secure with a few stitches.

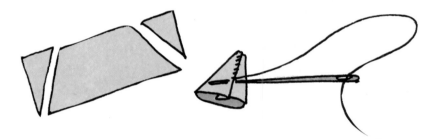

8 Trace the template on page 112 and cut out the doll's top from felt or fabric. Embroider a few stitches on the front to decorate. Fold it in half and sew up the side seams. Place the top onto the doll and secure the back with a couple of stitches in a contrasting color.

9 Cut a piece of ⅝-in. (1.5-cm) wide ribbon to approx. 2¾ in. (7 cm) long for the skirt. With right sides together, fold it in half and sew a seam about ¼ in. (5 mm) in from the edge. Turn right sides out and sew a line of running stitch across the top edge of the tube.

10 Place the skirt onto the doll, drawing the line of stitching in tight and placing a few stitches to secure it to the body, under the doll's top. Repeat this with a slightly longer piece of ribbon measuring 3 × 1¼ in. (8 × 3 cm), placing it under the first skirt and reaching down to the feet, to give you a two-tiered skirt.

Folk doll

Mix and match a selection of fabrics in florals, stripes, and dots to make this charming folk doll. She would make a very sweet gift for someone special, if you can bear to part with her!

Materials

Templates on page 113

2 pieces of patterned fabric, 5 × 3½ in. (12 × 9 cm), for the body

8 pieces of patterned fabric, 5 × 3 in. (12 × 7.5 cm), for the body

Sewing machine and matching sewing thread

4½ × 4½ in. (11 × 11 cm) fabric, for the apron

Tracing paper and pencil

Air-erasable marker pen

Batting (wadding), for stuffing

4 pieces of solid (plain) fabric, 3½ × 1¾ in. (9 × 4.5 cm), for the arms

4 pieces of patterned fabric, 3½ × 1¾ in. (9 × 4.5 cm), for the arms

A strip of felt, 10 × ¼ in. (25 cm × 5 mm) or felt string, for the hair

A small scrap of felt, for the face

Stranded embroidery floss (cotton) in blue, pink, and red

2 small buttons

1 For the back body section, take one of the larger rectangles of fabric and four of the smaller rectangles. With right sides facing and taking a ½ in. (1 cm) seam allowance, pin and machine stitch them together along the 5 in. (12 cm) width, to make a long strip. Trim the seam allowances and press the seams flat.

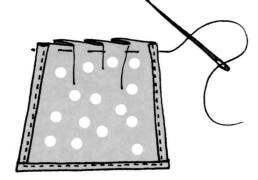

2 To make the apron, take the square piece of fabric and fold over a small double hem on three sides. Pin and machine stitch, then press. Make a few tucks along the top raw edge, so that it measures approx. 2 in. (5 cm) across. Pin, then baste (tack) to hold the tucks.

3 For the front body section, machine stitch three of the smaller pieces of fabric together as you did for the back section in step 1. Sew the larger rectangle of fabric to the remaining smaller piece in the same way.

4 Place the strip of three rectangles right way up on your work surface. Position the apron right way up on the fabric strip, aligning the top edge of the apron with the shorter raw edge of the strip, centering it between each side edge. With right side facing down, place the strip of two fabrics on top, matching the edge of the smaller rectangle with the edge of the apron. Pin and machine stitch together across the shorter edge. Trim the seam allowance and press.

5 Enlarge the template for the body on page 113 by 200 percent. Trace and cut out a paper template. Pin the template to the back section, draw around the shape with an air-erasable marker, and cut out. Repeat on the front section, taking care to tuck the apron out of the way when you cut out the shape.

6 For the hair, take the strip of felt and fold it into three loops. Secure the loops with a few stitches.

7 With right sides facing, pin the back and front pieced sections together, sandwiching the loops between the two pieces, with the tops of the loops facing down inside and the sewn end just poking out at the raw edge at the top of the head. Machine stitch all around the body, taking a ½-in. (1-cm) seam, leaving a 2½-in. (6-cm) gap in the seam on one long side.

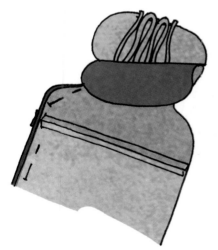

8 Turn right side out and stuff the doll with small pieces of batting (wadding), making sure there is plenty of batting in the neck area. Fold in the raw edges along the gap and slipstitch together.

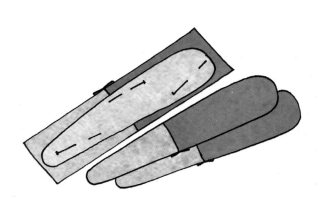

9 Enlarge the arm template on page 113 by 200 percent. Trace and cut out a paper template and pin the template to one of the arm pieces, making sure that the wider part of the arm is positioned on the patterned section. Draw around it and cut out. Repeat for all the arm pieces.

10 Take two of the arm pieces and with right sides together, pin and sew a ½-in. (1-cm) seam around the edge, leaving a 1¼-in. (3-cm) gap in the seam. Trim the seam allowances. Turn right sides out and stuff the arm, using the handle of a small paintbrush to push the stuffing up into the thin ends. Turn the raw edges in along the seam and slipstitch the gap closed.

11 Cut a small oval of felt for the face. Embroider the mouth with two small bullion knots, some tiny straight stitches for the cheeks, and a small bullion knot for each eye. Pin the oval to the head and sew around the edge using small appliqué stitch.

12 Position the arms on either side of the body, with the upper part of the arm extending ½ in. (1 cm) above the shoulder. Secure with a few stitches. Finally, sew two tiny buttons to the doll's bodice.

Appliquéd round pillow

I love the strikingly beautiful patterns on traditional Uzbekistan textiles. With the use of strong, vibrant colors, the bold circular and spiraled designs work well in a contemporary interior. Use wool felt or a mix of wool and man-made fiber. Acrylic felts do not hold a good shape and tend to tear at points of pressure.

Materials

To fit a 16-in. (40-cm) pillow form (cushion pad)

Motif on page 113

Newspaper

Pencil

String

Drawing pin

Masking tape

Tracing paper

Air-erasable marker pen

½ yd (½ m) cream felt

20 × 20 in. (50 × 50 cm) dark felt

Continuous zipper, approx. 20 in. (50 cm)

Sewing machine with zipper foot

Matching sewing thread

Round pillow form (cushion pad), 16 in. (40 cm) diameter

1 To make the circle template, cut out a piece of newspaper 18 × 18 in. (46 × 46 cm). Fold in half and half again. Open up and mark the center. Secure a piece of string with a drawing pin at this center point. Use masking tape to attach the other end of the string to a pencil, near the lead, so that when the string is held taut the lead reaches the edge of the paper at the end of a fold line. Keeping the string taut, swing the pencil around to draw a circle 18 in. (46 cm) in diameter. Use this template to cut out the front of the cushion from felt.

2 To make the two sections for the back, fold the template in half and trace around the semicircle on newspaper, adding ½ in. (1 cm) along the straight edge. Cut out the template and use this to cut two pieces of felt.

3 Enlarge the appliqué shapes on page 113 by 135 percent. Trace and cut them out to make templates that you can use to draw around on the cream felt. Cut out the felt pieces.

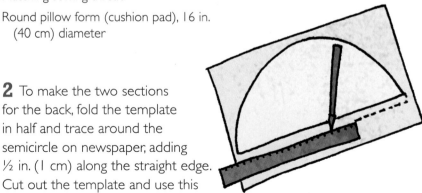

4 Start with the center shape. Pin it in position and then machine topstitch all around close to the edge. Following the guide on page 113, position the remaining pieces of felt, pin, and machine stitch in place.

5 To attach the zipper, lay the length of continuous zipper facing up on a flat surface. Take one of the back pieces and lay it over the zipper with the wrong side facing up, lining up the top edge with the top of the zipper. Pin in position and using a zipper foot, machine stitch approx. ⅜ in. (8 mm) down from the top edge. You want the line of stitching to be closer to the teeth of the zipper than to the edge but not so close that the zipper gets caught in the fabric. Turn the zipper and fabric over, fold back the fabric, and press.

6 Place the remaining back piece of fabric wrong side up over the top of the first piece, lining up the top edge of the fabric with the top edge of the zipper. Pin and sew a line of stitching as you did for the other side.

7 Open up the zipper halfway and, with right sides together, pin the front piece and the back piece together. Sew all around, making sure that the two ends of the zipper that are open are lying flat and close to each other.

8 Trim off the excess ends of the zipper. Turn the pillow right side out, press, and insert the pillow form (cushion pad).

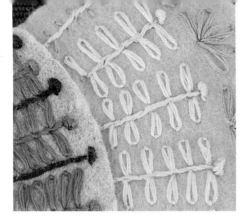

Indian peacock chair pad

The national bird of India features throughout Indian mythology. Indian craftsmen depict its graceful form in paintings and wood carvings, and in beautiful embroidered silks and colorful kantha folk art quilts. Use bright embroidery floss on a vibrant orange fabric to transform a simple child's chair into an exotic throne fit for royalty!

Materials

Motif and stitch guide on page 113

Scraps of colored felt

Air-erasable marker pen

Dressmaker's carbon paper

19 × 17 ½ in. (48 × 44 cm) main cotton fabric

9½ × 8¾ in. (24 × 22 cm) cotton batting (wadding)

Stranded embroidery floss (cotton) in assorted bright colors

48 in. (120 cm) cotton tape or ribbon

1 Enlarge the shapes that make up the body of the peacock on page 113 by 200 percent and use them to cut out the pieces from different colored felt.

2 Cut the main fabric in half to make two rectangles, 9½ × 8¾ in. (24 × 22 cm). Pin the top part of the tail section to the right side of the front piece, positioning it 1½ in. (4 cm) in from the right edge and 3¼ in. (8 cm) up from the bottom. Pin the other sections in place following the guide. Use appliqué stitch to secure the sections to the fabric around all edges.

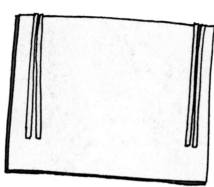

3 Use an air-erasable marker to draw in the straight lines that make up part of the design. You could use dressmaker's carbon paper but sometimes it is easier to follow the guide and draw them in by eye. Follow the stitch guide on page 113 to embroider the patterns and the branch design the peacock is standing on.

4 Place the front section with the embroidery facing up on a flat surface. Place the cotton batting on top of this, lining up all the edges. Cut the tape into 4 equal lengths, each approx 12 in. (30 cm) long. Place two pieces of tape 1¼ in. (3 cm) in from each corner on the top edge, with the tapes extending down into the inside and the ends flush with the top edge of the batting and front piece.

5 Place the back piece of fabric right side down on top of the batting, with the ties sandwiched in between, and pin in place. Machine stitch around the edge, taking a ½-in. (1-cm) seam and leaving a 2¾-in. (7-cm) gap in the seam to turn the cushion the right side out.

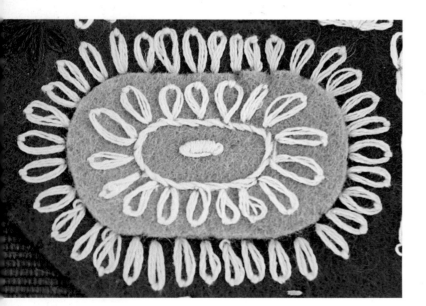

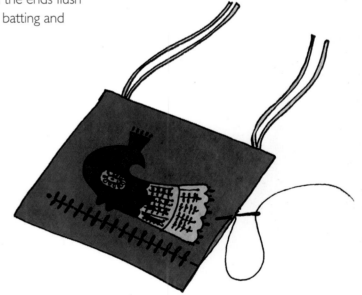

6 Trim the seam allowance and cut across the corners. Turn right side out. Turn in the raw edges along the gap and slipstitch the gap closed.

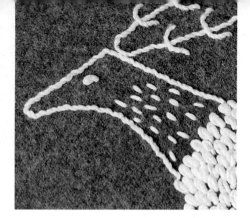

Reindeer pillow

Pillows are a great way of changing the look of a room and bringing warmth and pattern to your interiors. This example is influenced by the wonderfully organic designs that are the essence of folk art. The white stitching on the soft-gray felted wool creates a particularly striking effect.

Materials

To fit a 12 × 20-in. (30 × 50-cm) pillow form (cushion pad):

Motifs and stitch guides on page 114

18½ × 12¼ in. (46 × 32 cm) gray felted wool

Dressmaker's carbon paper

White stranded embroidery floss (cotton) or knitting yarn

4¾ × 2 in. (12 × 5 cm) yellow felt for label

26½ × 23¼ in. (66 × 58 cm) white woolen fabric

Pillow form (cushion pad), 12 × 20 in. (30 × 50 cm)

1 Enlarge the design on page 114 by 200 percent and, using dressmaker's carbon paper, transfer it onto the gray front piece. Center the design between the two long edges and 2¾ in. (7 cm) in from the shorter left-hand edge. Follow the stitch guide on page 114 and embroider the design onto the fabric.

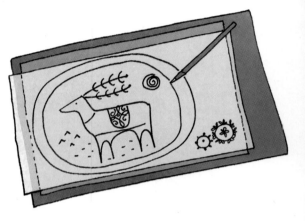

2 To make the label, transfer the design onto one end of the yellow fabric piece using dressmaker's carbon paper. Follow the stitch guide to embroider the pattern. Fold the rectangle in half and machine stitch along the two side edges and outer edge of the label, keeping the stitching close to the edge.

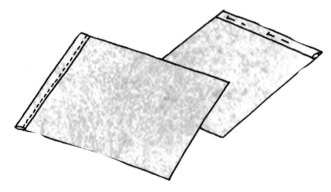

3 From the white fabric, cut one rectangle measuring 13½ × 12¼ in. (34 × 32 cm) and one measuring 12¼ × 10½ in. (32 × 26 cm). Take one piece and fold in a ½-in. (1-cm) double hem along one 12¼ in. (32 cm) edge. Pin and machine stitch the hem. Press and repeat with the other piece.

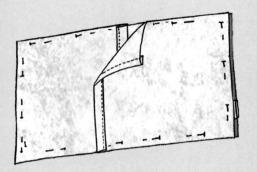

4 Place the front section with the right side facing up on your work surface. Position the two back pieces right side down, so that the hemmed edges face the center, with the larger piece overlapping. Sandwich the label with the design facing down, in between the front and back section on the side edge. Pin in position so that the label edge aligns with the raw edges of the pillow.

5 Machine stitch all around the edge of the pillow, taking a ½-in. (1-cm) seam. Trim the seam allowance and snip across each corner. Turn right side out through the envelope back and press. Insert the pillow form (cushion pad).

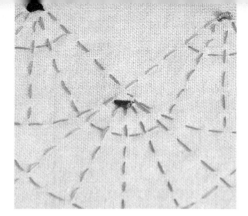

Sashiko play mat

This reversible play mat has a comfy inner layer of cotton batting, so makes a lovely cloth to place a baby on. The border and quilting stitch is sashiko, a decorative and functional stitch from Japan. Originally it was used to mend and reinforce items of clothing, but on quilts it provides decoration and holds the layers together.

Materials

Motif and stitch guide on page 114

24 × 21¾ in. (60 × 55 cm) solid (plain) fabric, such as natural linen, for the borders

Two 24½ × 21¾-in. (62 × 55-cm) pieces of patterned cotton fabric for the main panels—as the mat is reversible you could choose a different fabric for each side

Dressmaker's carbon paper

Air-erasable marker pen

Stranded embroidery floss (cotton) in assorted colors

36 × 21¾ in. (90 × 55 cm) cotton batting (wadding)

Sewing machine

Matching sewing thread

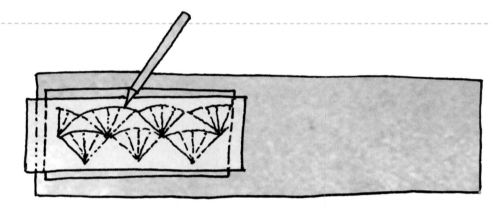

1 Cut the border fabric into 4 rectangles, 6 × 21¾ in. (15 × 55 cm) each. Enlarge the sashiko pattern on page 114 by 135 percent and, using dressmaker's carbon paper, transfer the design onto two of the border pieces, positioning the pattern 1¼ in. (3 cm) down from the top edge.

2 Stitch the sashiko pattern following the guide on page 114. Place a bullion knot at the point of each fan shape. Complete both ends of the border pieces.

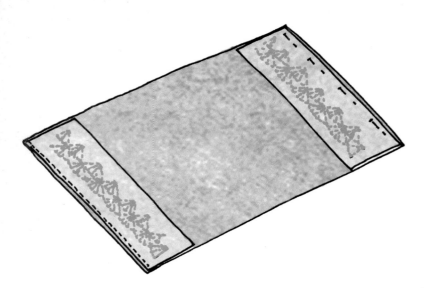

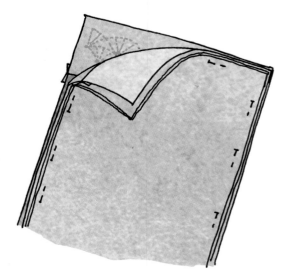

3 With right sides together, pin the two border pieces to the ends of the top main fabric piece. Machine stitch together, taking a ½-in. (1-cm) seam. Trim the seam allowance and press. Repeat to add the plain border pieces to the main back panel.

4 Place the front and back panels together with right sides facing. Position the piece of cotton batting (wadding) on the top. Pin and baste (tack) the three layers together, trimming any excess batting so that the raw edges are aligned.

5 Machine stitch the four sides, taking a ½-in. (1-cm) seam and leaving a gap of approx. 6 in. (15 cm) in the seam to turn the mat right side out.

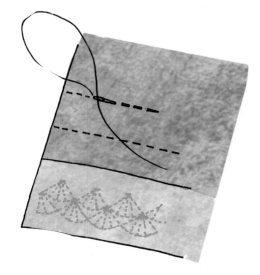

6 Trim the seam allowance, remove the basting (tacking), and cut across each corner, then turn the mat right side out through the gap. Turn in the raw edges and slipstitch the gap closed.

7 Use a ruler and air-erasable marker to mark lines at 4-in. (10-cm) intervals across the width of the mat on the main fabric panel. Follow the lines to stitch rows of sashiko across the panels, taking the needle through the side seam to hide the end of thread in the crease.

Hand-tied quilt

In India, vintage saris are used to make beautifully colored quilts, hand stitched with small running stitches. Another way to secure the layers is by hand tying. I have used this method here with different colored threads—it is very quick and easy and adds a stylish design element to the quilt.

Materials

12 squares of cotton in contrasting fabrics, 9½ × 9½ in. (24 × 24 cm)

35½ × 26¾ in. (90 × 68 cm), solid (plain) backing fabric

2 strips of fabric, 3 × 26¾ in. (8 × 68 cm)

2 strips of fabric, 3 × 36¼ in. (8 × 92 cm)

35½ × 26¾ in. (90 × 68 cm), cotton batting (wadding)

Stranded embroidery floss (cotton) in different colors

Air-erasable marker pen

Sewing machine and matching sewing thread

1 Lay the squares of fabric on a flat surface in three rows of four, moving them around until you are happy with the arrangement and mix of colors. Working one row at a time, pin the squares right sides together with a ½-in. (1-cm) seam. Machine stitch and press the seams to one side. Complete four rows.

2 With right sides together and aligning the seams, pin the three rows together. Machine stitch a ½-in. (1-cm) seam across the rows. Press the seams to one side.

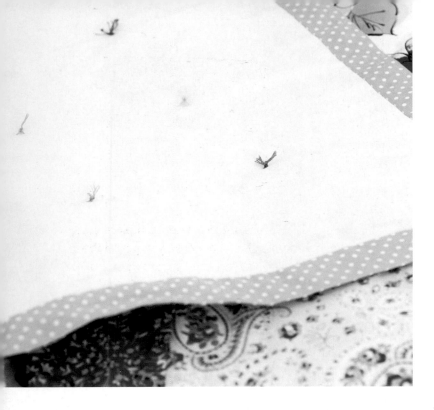

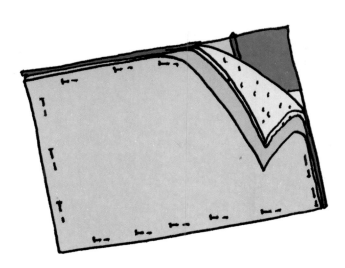

3 Lay the pieced squares right side down on a flat surface, with the wadding on top. Place the backing fabric on top right side up, aligning the edges. Pin and then baste (tack) the three layers together.

4 With the squared side facing up, take one of the shorter border strips and with right side down, pin it to the shorter width of the quilt, aligning the raw edges. Machine stitch, taking a ½-in. (1-cm) seam. Repeat for the opposite edge.

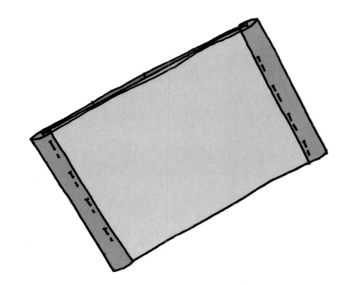

5 Turn the quilt over. Fold the strip in half and fold under a ½-in. (1-cm) hem and pin in position. Repeat with the opposite edge.

6 Repeat steps 4 and 5 for the longer side edges but this time fold in each end of the strip by ½ in. (1 cm) before pinning the strip to the edge of the quilt.

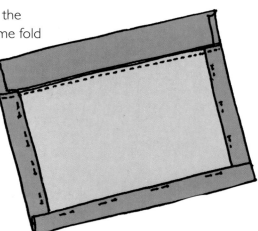

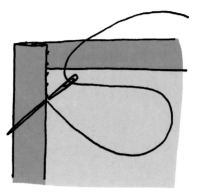

7 Hand stitch the strips in place using appliqué stitch. When you get to the corners, close the gap at the end of the strip with a few small stitches.

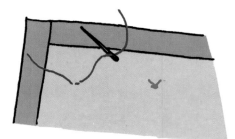

8 With an air-erasable pen, mark the position of the hand-tied knot in the center of each square. Thread a needle with a piece of embroidery floss approx. 8 in. (20 cm) long. Push the needle through the center mark on the squared side, taking the needle through all three layers and to the reverse side. Bring the needle up again through the three layers approx. ⅛ in. (3 mm) away from where the thread emerged.

9 Making sure both thread ends are roughly equal in length, remove the needle and tie a double knot. Trim the ends to approx. ⅝ in. (1.5 cm) long. Repeat steps 8 and 9 to tie knots in all the squares. Press.

Picnic cloth

The design on this picnic cloth is worked in cross stitch, a form of embroidery that has been used all over the world for many centuries. The simple stitch, embroidered in shades of pink, epitomizes folksy charm, but using big stitches on crisp blue and white gingham brings it right up to date.

Materials

Stitch guide on page 114

16½ × 16½ in. (42 × 42 cm) gingham fabric

17 × 17 in. (43 × 43 cm) backing fabric

Stranded embroidery floss (cotton) in white, pale pink, dark pink, red, bright green, and light green

Sewing machine and matching sewing thread

1 Enlarge the stitch guide on page 114 by 155 percent and follow the guide to work the rose design in cross stitch in one corner of the gingham, placing the design approx. 3¼ in. (8 cm) in from each edge.

2 Fold over a single ¾-in. (2-cm) hem all around the edge of the backing fabric. Press and pin in place. At each corner fold back one end of the fabric into a triangle to miter the corner for a neat finish (see page 123).

3 Fold back a ½-in. (1-cm) hem on the gingham fabric and, starting at one corner with the wrong sides together, pin the front section to the back, ½ in. (1 cm) in from the edge of the backing fabric to reveal a small border. Machine stitch all around to secure the front and back together.

I have used a thin oilcloth as a backing fabric, but floral cotton would work just as well.

Tulip seat cover

I have made a pretty cover for a stool but you could easily adapt the design to fit a chair. The simple cover uses the tulip motif that appears in traditional embroidery from Eastern Europe. Sewn in green and blue on stripy ticking, it has a fresh, country appeal.

Materials

Motif and stitch guide on page 115

Stool

Ruler

Set square

Cotton ticking or stripy fabric

Green and blue stranded embroidery floss (cotton)

Air-erasable marker pen

Tracing paper

Dressmaker's carbon paper

Sewing machine

Matching sewing thread

1 Make a template for your stool. Measure the top of the stool, add ⅝ in. (1.5 cm) all around, and draw the square or rectangle onto a large sheet of paper or newspaper, using a set square. Draw a 3½-in. (9-cm) border all around. Extend the lines that make up the inner square or rectangle out from each corner to meet the outer square or rectangle.

2 Cut out the template and cut away and discard the drawn squares at each corner. Pin the template to the stripy fabric (making sure that it is aligned with any stripes) and cut out the shape.

3 Enlarge the design on page 115 by 200 percent and transfer it using dressmaker's carbon paper to the center of the fabric. Follow the stitch guide to embroider the design.

The cover uses the tulip motif that appears in traditional embroidery from Eastern Europe.

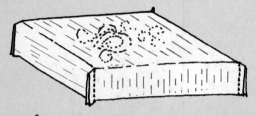

4 Place the embroidered piece right side down on a flat surface. With right sides together, line up the two raw edges at each corner and pin to form the sides that will fit over the top of the stool—you will create a box shape. Sew a ½-in. (1-cm) seam at each corner. Trim the seam allowance and press.

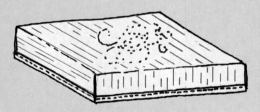

5 Turn under a ½-in. (1-cm) double hem all the way around the edge, pin, and baste (tack) in place. Machine stitch the hem, remove the basting, and press. Turn right side out.

Spanish fish tablecloth

Bring some Mediterranean sunshine to your table setting with this jumping fish design, embroidered in vibrant blue and green. Based on the rustic pottery of the Catalan region of Northern Spain, it is perfect for a summer meal of little dishes of tapas.

Materials

Motif and stitch guide on page 115

24½ × 24½ in. (62 × 62 cm) piece of linen

Stranded embroidery floss (cotton) in dark green, light green, dark blue, and light blue

Dressmaker's carbon paper

Sewing machine

Matching sewing thread

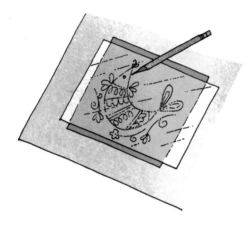

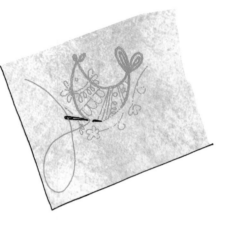

1 Enlarge the fish motif on page 115 by 155 percent and transfer it onto the corner of your fabric using dressmaker's carbon paper, positioning the design 4 in. (10 cm) in from the edges.

2 Follow the stitch guide on page 115 to embroider the design in the different colors.

3 Fold over and pin a ½ in. (1-cm) double hem all around the four sides of the cloth. Machine stitch the hem and press to finish.

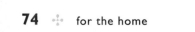

Little bird letter rack

I love working with thick, natural wool felts. The making of felt is an ancient tradition and in some parts of the world it still forms a strong part of nomadic culture. In Central and Eastern Asia, rugs, tents, and clothing were all made in felt and felt-making is still practiced and in use today.

Materials

*Makes a container measuring approx.
6 x 4 x 3¼ in. (15 x 10 x 8 cm)*

Motif and stitch guide on page 115

Approx. 23½ x 6 in. (60 x 15 cm) or 3 x 8-in. (20-cm) square sheets of gray wool felt, ¼ in. (5 mm) thick—if you can't find thick felt simply add a fraction of an inch to each side of the base to fit

Gray, red, and white stranded embroidery floss (cotton)

Air-erasable marker pen

1 Cut the following from the felt: two rectangles 4 x 6 in. (10 x 15 cm) for front and back panels; two rectangles 4 x 3¼ in. (10 x 8 cm) for side panels; and one rectangle 5½ x 2¾ in. (14 x 7 cm) for base.

2 Natural felt is quite difficult to draw on to mark out your design. The easiest way to transfer the stitch motif is to cut out the outline shape of the bird on page 115 from paper. Pin this to the front panel and draw around it with an air-erasable marker. Copy the stitch patterns and twig by eye—it doesn't matter if they look slightly different to the one I have made.

3 Embroider the bird following the guide on page 115. On one of the side panels, sew a line of running stitch in gray stranded embroidery floss (cotton), ⅝ in. (1.5 cm) in from the right edge. Approx. ¼ in. (5 mm) to the side of this, sew a row of small bullion knots in white. Repeat on the other side panel but place the stitching on the left side of the panel.

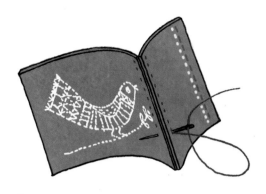

4 Take the front panel and one of the side panels and, with wrong sides together, pin the two edges together. Join the two panels together with a row of small bullion knots spaced approx. ½ in. (1 cm) apart, stitched in a contrasting color (red) to the base felt. To do this, make a bullion knot on one side of the seam, then take the needle through at the base of the knot to the adjoining panel, place a knot on this side, and take the needle back again ½ in. (1 cm) down the edge on the other side. Continue down the side. Repeat to attach the back panel and the other side panel.

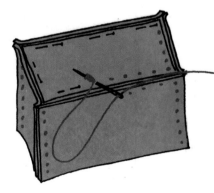

5 Pin the base rectangle in position, making sure all the edges line up with the side edges of the upright box shape. Stitch all the panels together with bullion knots as in step 4.

Pot holder

I have quite a collection of brightly colored retro china. I am drawn toward the folksy designs of the 60s and 70s and, although I rarely use a china coffee jug, I have a number of lovely pots on my shelves. The design on this cheery pot holder would fit in well with my growing collection!

Materials

Motif and stitch guide on page 116

Cotton batting (wadding)

8 × 6 in. (20 × 15 cm) solid (plain) turquoise cotton fabric for upper section

8 × 2¾ in. (20 × 7 cm) contrasting cotton fabric for lower section

Dressmaker's carbon paper

8-in. (20-cm) square cotton fabric for backing

Air-erasable marker pen

Dark blue and white stranded embroidery floss (cotton)

Approx. 1 yd (1 m) dark blue bias binding

Sewing machine

Matching sewing thread

1 Cut out the fabric pieces and cut an 8-in. (20-cm) square of batting (wadding). Enlarge the coffee pot design on page 116 by 155 percent and, using dressmaker's carbon paper, transfer it onto the piece of turquoise cotton for the front.

2 Following the stitch guide on page 116, embroider the design for the coffee pot on the turquoise fabric for the upper section.

3 You can use any fabric as a contrast to the upper section of the pot holder. My fabric already had a stitch effect on it. If you want to achieve the same look, stitch three rows of running stitch ⅝ in. (1.5 cm) apart and starting ⅝ in. (1.5 cm) up from the base. Vary the length of stitch and change the thickness of the stitch by using the embroidery floss (cotton) single or double.

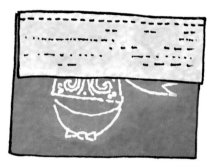

4 With right sides facing, pin the two front sections together along the bottom edge of the turquoise fabric. Machine stitch together, taking a ½-in. (1-cm) seam. Trim the seam allowance and press flat.

5 Place the embroidered front piece right side down on your work surface. Place the square of batting (wadding) on top and finally add the square of backing fabric, right side facing out. Pin the three layers together.

6 Machine stitch four evenly spaced lines, ⅝ in. (1.5 cm) apart and starting ½ in. (1 cm) up from the bottom edge, across the bottom section of the front panel to quilt it. Trim all the four corners into a curve, taking care not to cut into the stitching.

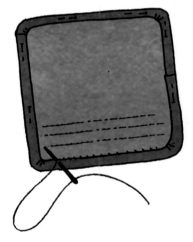

7 To make the contrasting edge, cut a length of bias binding that is long enough to go all around the pot holder with an extra 1 in. (2 cm) to fold over at the end. Open out the bias binding flat and with right sides together and edges aligned, pin it around the edge of the pot holder. Machine stitch in place, stitching along the fold of the bias binding. When you have come nearly full circle, overlap the start by ½ in. (1 cm) and turn under ½ in. (1 cm) to make a neat finish. Continue stitching to the end.

8 Fold the bias binding over to the back of the pot holder. Pin in place, making sure that the raw edge of the binding is folded under. Use small slipstitches to sew the bias binding to the back.

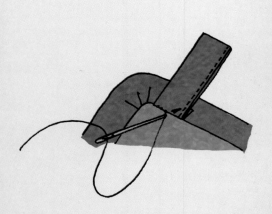

9 To make the hanging loop, cut a small piece of bias binding 4 in. (10 cm) long. Machine stitch the open edges together and fold in the bottom raw edges by approx. ¼ in. (5 mm). Fold the strip in half and hand stitch the ends to the back top right-hand corner of the pot holder. Press.

The design on this cheery pot holder would fit in well with any kitchen!

Coasters

I have used scraps of handblocked Indian fabrics in rich earthy colors for these useful coasters. They are so easy to make, sewn with a simple running stitch—the same method as Indian kantha quilts—and will be a stylish addition to any dining table or a great house-warming gift.

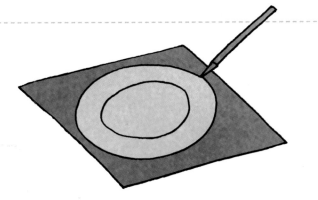

Materials

Round plate, approx. 7 in. (18 cm) diameter, to draw around

Scraps of fabric in toning colors

Air-erasable marker pen

Sewing machine

Matching sewing thread

Stranded embroidery floss (cotton) in toning colors

1 Use the plate as a template to draw around on the fabric and cut out two circles for each coaster.

2 Pin the two circles together with wrong sides facing. Machine stitch around the circle, taking a ½-in. (1-cm) seam, leaving a gap of approx. 1½ in. (3.5 cm) in the seam for turning through.

3 Trim the seam allowance and cut slits around the edge to ease the shape (see page 122). Turn right side out. Turn in the raw edges at the gap and sew the gap closed with small slipstitches.

4 The coasters are reversible so to prevent any knots showing, take the needle into the middle of the two pieces of fabric without tying a knot in the end of your embroidery floss (cotton), about 2 in. (5 cm) away from where you want to start your stitching. Bring the needle out ½ in. (1 cm) in from the outer edge. Pull the thread through and as the end of the thread just disappears into the middle of the two layers, stop. Make your first running stitch and go back over it to make a double stitch. Continue to sew a row of running stitch around the circle.

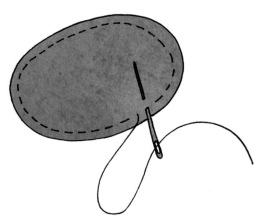

5 When you have finished one row, bring the needle out ½ in. (1 cm) in from the first row, and work another circle of running stitches. Continue adding a circle of running stitch, moving in ½ in. (1 cm) at a time.

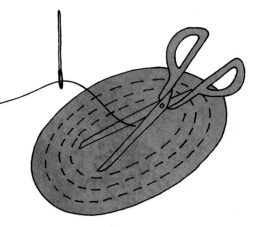

6 When you need to renew the thread, go over your last stitch twice, take the needle into the middle between the two layers and come up to the front of the fabric about 2½ in. (6 cm) away. Snip the thread close to the fabric so that the end disappears back between the two layers. Finish the center with a seed stitch.

Stripy table mat

With simple, bold stitching in thick yarn and bordered with matching pompoms, this table mat has a lovely rustic appeal. I used a woven stripy, woolen fabric but you could use cotton ticking or plain felted wool. To make a table runner, simply increase the length and repeat the stitching at equal intervals.

Materials

Stitch guide on page 116

Approx. 24 × 15 in. (60 × 38 cm) stripy fabric

Tapestry yarn in different colors

Blunt-ended needle

Air-erasable marker pen (optional)

Sewing machine

Matching sewing thread

31½ in. (80 cm) pompom trimming

1 The fabric I used has a 1-in. (2.5-cm) stripe and I have embroidered approx. 5 in. (12 cm) long rows of stitches into each white stripe—adapt the measurements to suit your fabric. If your fabric has thinner stripes, you could work every third stripe or, if your fabric is solid (plain), use an air-erasable marker to mark out seven evenly spaced 5-in. (12-cm) lines across the width.

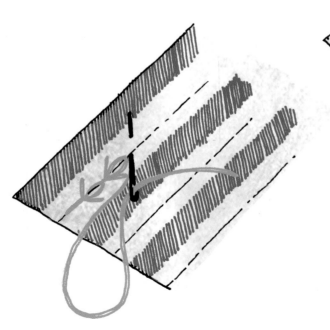

2 Follow the stitch guide on page 116 to embroider the rows of stitches on both ends of the panel. Start the rows of stitching approx. 1½ in. (3.5 cm) in from each edge to allow for a hem.

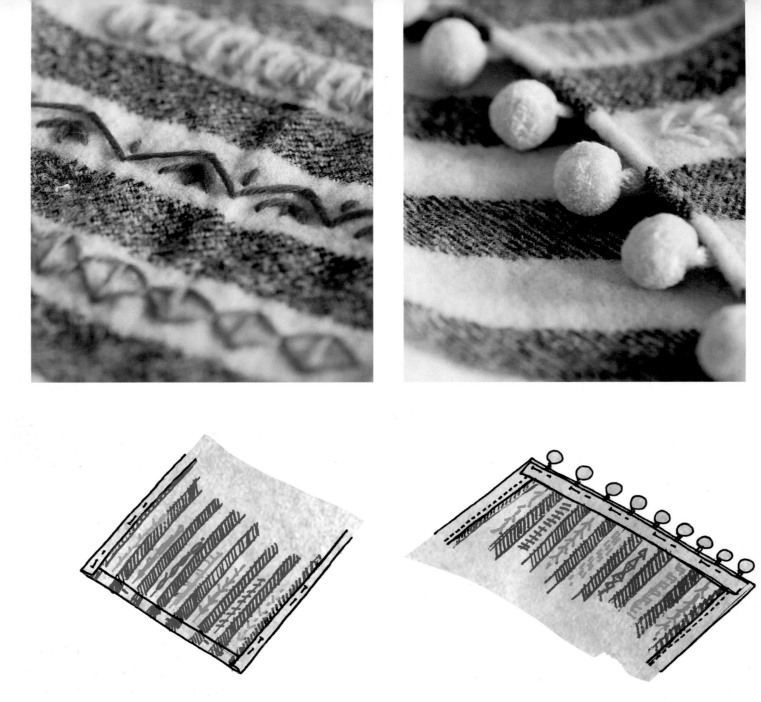

3 Turn under a ½-in. (1-cm) double hem on all four sides of the table mat and pin in place. Machine stitch all around.

4 Pin a length of pompom trimming to either end of the mat. Lining up the top of the pompom tape with the edge of the cloth on the under side. Stitch in place, either by hand or machine.

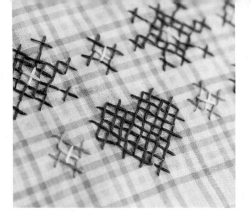

Hanky pocket apron

There is no reason why you shouldn't look gorgeous while doing mundane kitchen tasks like scrubbing dishes. I have used an elegant dish towel that I always thought too good for drying up and, keeping the recycled theme going, I embroidered a handkerchief with a pretty scalloped edge for the pocket.

Materials

Motif and stitch guide on page 116

A handkerchief or checked fabric, approx. 15 × 8 in. (38 × 20 cm)

Stranded embroidery floss (cotton) in pink, blue, and white

A dish (tea) towel

2 yd (2 m) cotton tape, 1½ in. (3.5 cm) wide

1 The embroidery is worked in cross stitch. Enlarge the motif on page 116 by 155 percent. Follow the guide to stitch the pattern, placing the design 2¾ in. (7 cm) up from the base of the handkerchief or piece of fabric and an equal distance from each side.

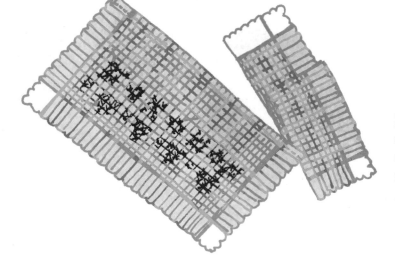

2 If you are using a handkerchief, cut a strip from the top edge so that the fabric measures 6½ in. (16 cm) deep. Turn over a double ½-in. (1-cm) hem along the raw edge and machine stitch. If you are using a piece of fabric, turn over a ½-in. (1-cm) hem on all 4 sides, pin, and machine stitch.

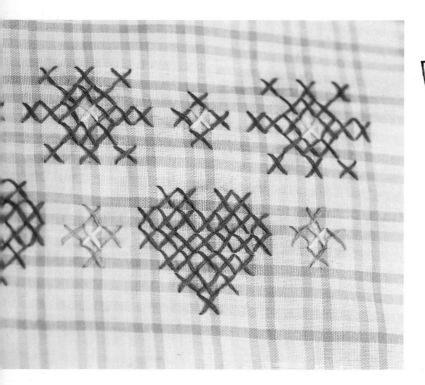

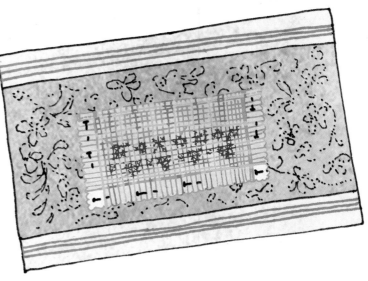

3 Pin the pocket to the dish (tea) towel, positioning it approx. 6 in. (15 cm) up from the bottom edge, centered between each side edge. Either machine or hand stitch the pocket in place along the three hemmed edges.

4 Turn the dish towel over and pin the length of cotton tape to the inside top, lining up the edge of the tape with the top edge of the dish towel and making sure there is an equal length of tape extending out on either side to make the ties. Machine stitch along the top and bottom edge of the tape and across the width at each side edge of the dish towel.

Jar cover

Everyone loves to receive home-made jam or jelly as a gift. Why not make it that bit more special with a hand-embroidered cover? Secure it with a pretty gingham ribbon to complete the homespun, country charm.

Materials

Motifs and stitch guide on page 117

Round plate, approx. 13 in. (33 cm) diameter, to draw around

6 × 6 in. (15 × 15 cm) linen or cotton fabric

Tracing paper and pencil

Air-erasable marker pen

Dressmaker's carbon paper

Stranded embroidery floss (cotton) in dark pink, lighter pink, green, blue, and yellow

Sewing machine and matching sewing thread

Approx. 16 in. (40 cm) ribbon

A conserve jar or pot

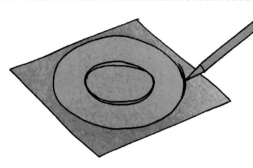

1 Use the plate as a template to draw around on the fabric and cut out the circle.

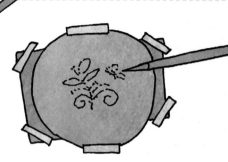

2 Transfer the design on page 117 onto the center of the circle using dressmaker's carbon paper or, if your fabric is light colored, the light box or window tracing method (see page 121).

3 Embroider the design following the stitch guide on page 117. The raspberry is made of bullion knots—I used embroidery floss that was a mix of dark and lighter pink, which adds a pretty detail.

4 Use a sewing machine set to a tight zigzag to stitch around the circle, close to the edge. I have chosen to match the sewing thread to the color of the linen but you could pick out one of the colors from the embroidery. Secure the cover to the jar lid with the ribbon to finish.

Pillowcase

Making a pretty pillowcase is a good way of giving a new lease of life to a plain bed linen set. I have used a tiny gingham check and red, white, and blue stitching for a folksy look that is charming but also stylish and contemporary.

Materials

Motif and stitch guide on page 117

66 × 20½ in. (168 × 52 cm) cotton fabric

Sewing machine

Matching sewing thread

Dressmaker's carbon paper

Embroidery floss (cotton) in red, white, and blue

1 Cut the fabric into two pieces, one measuring 31½ × 20½ in. (80 × 52 cm) and one measuring 34½ × 20½ in. (88 × 52 cm). On the smaller piece, turn under a ½-in. (1-cm) hem, press, and then turn under a 2½-in. (6-cm) hem along the width at one end. Pin and machine stitch.

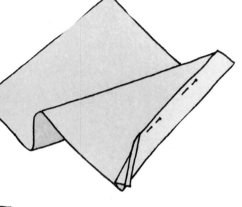

2 On the larger piece of fabric, turn under a ½-in. (1-cm) double hem across the width at one end. Pin and machine stitch.

3 Transfer the design from page 117 to the center of the smaller piece using dressmaker's carbon paper. Embroider the design following the stitch guide.

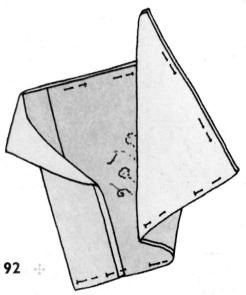

4 With right sides facing, pin the back and front pieces together, aligning the raw edges along the bottom and two long sides. Fold back the hemmed end of the longer side so that it is the same length as the front panel.

5 Machine stitch along the side and bottom edges, taking a ½-in. (1-cm) seam. Zigzag stitch the raw edges. Turn the pillowcase right side out and press.

Gingham check and red, white, and blue stitching create a folksy look that is charming but also stylish.

Teacup pincushion

I found a set of these cups and saucers in my local thrift store. I love the design, with the charming little folksy scene in blue and pink. It was just right to make into this useful and pretty pincushion, an essential addition to any sewing table. Teacup pincushions are so simple to make and the perfect gift for a crafty friend.

Materials

Motif and stitch guide on page 117

Teacup and saucer

Approx. 8-in. (20-cm) square piece of cotton or linen fabric

Compass or 7 in. (18 cm) diameter household object

Air-erasable marker pen

Dressmaker's carbon paper

Blue stranded embroidery floss (cotton)

Sewing needle and strong cotton thread

Fiberfill (polyester) stuffing

Glue (optional)

1 My teacup is 3 in. (8 cm) in diameter; if your teacup is smaller adjust the measurements of the circle to fit. Draw a circle onto your fabric with a diameter of 7 in. (18 cm), either using a compass or something round of a similar size, such as a plate or saucepan lid. Cut out the circle.

2 Use dressmaker's carbon paper to transfer the motif on page 117 onto the center of the circle. Follow the stitch guide to embroider the design.

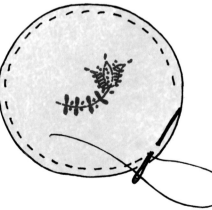

3 Thread a sewing needle with strong cotton thread and double the thread for strength. Sew a line of running stitch all around the circle, approx. ¼ in. (5 mm) in from the edge.

4 Pull the end of the thread so that the circle gathers up into a ball shape. When the opening is approx. 2 in. (5 cm) wide, tie off the end of the thread. Stuff the circle with small amounts of stuffing until you have a nice firm ball.

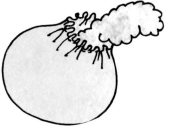

5 Push the pincushion down into the cup until it is firmly in place. You can glue it into position if you like.

Lavender bag

Beautifully scented lavender bags make a wonderful gift. Either hang the bag in a closet or keep it near your pillow at night—lavender pillows induce a calming effect to help you relax and sleep soundly. To make the stitching easy, use a fabric with a small check—gingham would look lovely, too.

Materials

Motif and stitch guide on page 118

6¼-in. (16-cm) square piece of squared or checked cotton or linen fabric

Small scrap of felt for the face

4 in. (10 cm) ribbon

Stranded embroidery floss (cotton) in two colors

Sewing machine

Matching sewing thread

Dried lavender

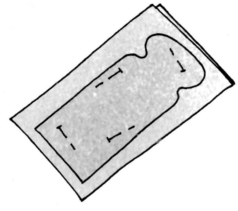

1 Trace the lavender bag template on page 118 and cut out the front and back pieces from the fabric and the face from felt.

2 Follow the stitch guide on page 118 to embroider the front of the body.

3 Place the front and back pieces with right sides together. Fold the length of ribbon in half and sandwich it between the front and back pieces, with the folded end facing inward and the raw edges aligned. Pin the layers together and machine stitch with a ½-in. (1-cm) seam, leaving a 1½-in. (3.5-cm) gap in the seam to turn right side out.

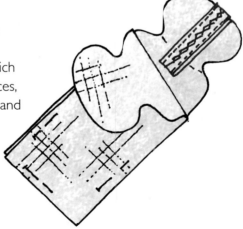

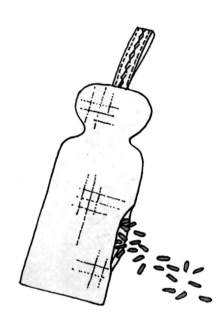

4 Trim the seam allowance and clip the curves and corners (see page 122). Turn right side out through the gap. Fill the shape with dried lavender until firm. Turn in the raw edges and slipstitch the gap closed.

5 Embroider the face following the guide on page 118 and sew it to the head using appliqué stitch. Embroider the hair using satin stitch.

Covered buttons

These gorgeous buttons are made using traditional motifs and have been stitched onto denim in striking red and white. They would make a lovely gift presented in a little box and could be used on anything from clothes or pillows to quilts or bags.

Materials

Motifs and stitch guides on page 118

Buttons measuring approx. 1¼ in. (3 cm) in diameter with central shank

Scraps of denim fabric, at least 2 × 2 in. (5 × 5 cm) for each button

Dressmaker's carbon paper

Red and white stranded embroidery floss (cotton)

Matching sewing thread

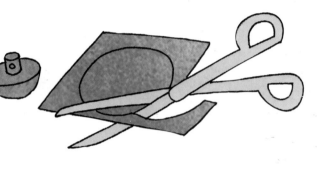

1 To cover a button measuring 1¼ in. (3 cm) in diameter, cut out some circles of fabric measuring 2 in. (5 cm) in diameter.

2 Using dressmaker's carbon paper, transfer a motif from page 118 onto the fabric, positioning the pattern in the center of the circle. Embroider the design following the stitch guide.

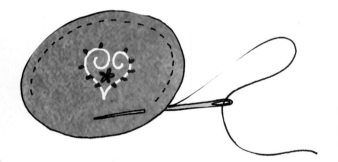

3 Thread a sewing needle with thread and sew a row of small running stitches all around the circle, ¼ in. (5 mm) in from the edge.

4 Place the circle over the front of the button and pull on the end of the thread to gather the material together. Secure the fabric in place by hand sewing from one side to the other, pulling the gathered fabric tight until the fabric is smooth.

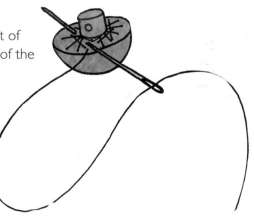

Covered notebook

An embroidered cover for a notebook is a great way of turning something that is quite ordinary into something very special. I have chosen a vibrant yellow fabric for the cover and my Indian inspired peacock is stitched in bright red for a striking look. Simply alter the measurements to fit any size notebook.

Materials

To cover a notebook measuring 5½ × 8 in. (14 × 20 cm) with a ¾ in. (2 cm) spine

Motif and stitch guide on page 119

Tracing paper and pencil

Dressmaker's carbon paper

9 × 16½ in. (23 × 42 cm) piece of fabric, felt, cotton, or linen are all suitable

Red stranded embroidery floss (cotton)

Sewing machine and matching sewing thread

A notebook, 5½ × 8 in. (14 × 20 cm)

1 To make a cover for a different-sized notebook, simply measure across the front and back, including the spine, and add approx. 5 in. (12 cm) to the width. Measure from the top to the bottom and add 1¼ in. (3 cm) to the depth. Cut out your fabric to these measurements.

2 Enlarge the peacock design on page 119 by 155 percent and use dressmaker's carbon paper to transfer the design onto the right side of the fabric, positioning it about 3¼ in. (8 cm) in from the right edge and centered between the side edges.

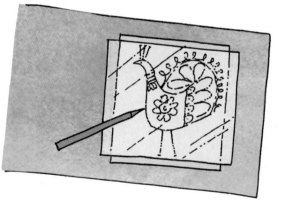

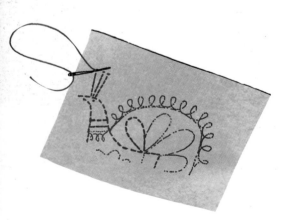

3 Embroider the peacock using backstitch and bullion knots following the stitch guide on page 119.

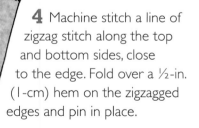

4 Machine stitch a line of zigzag stitch along the top and bottom sides, close to the edge. Fold over a ½-in. (1-cm) hem on the zigzagged edges and pin in place.

5 Turn over a double ½-in. (1-cm) hem along each side edge and machine stitch in place. Fold each side edge in to the wrong side by 2 in. (5 cm) and pin. Topstitch along the top and bottom edges close to the edge to secure the flaps. Slip the notebook under the flaps to finish.

Espadrilles

Originally peasant footwear made and worn in the Catalonian region of France and Spain since the 14th century, espadrilles have become hugely popular with thousands of styles available. I still love the original simple flat style and have worked a brightly colored design to complement the gorgeous pink canvas.

Materials

Motif and stitch guide on page 118

A pair of espadrilles

Tracing paper and pencil

Dressmaker's carbon paper

Stranded embroidery floss (cotton) in a variety of bright colors

1 Using embroidery floss (cotton), hand stitch one row of zigzag stitch across the front edge of the espadrille upper. Position a small French knot beneath the point of each zigzag.

2 Using dressmaker's carbon paper, transfer the motif on page 118 onto the front of one of the espadrilles. Follow the stitch guide to embroider the design and repeat to embroider the second shoe.

3 As it is quite difficult to finish off the thread when you are stitching down toward the toe, when you need to change the thread, bring the thread up through stitches on the inside and use the back of the zigzagged line to finish off.

Turreted house key ring

Hopefully with this brightly stitched key ring you won't constantly lose your keys (like me!). The turreted house design is straight out of a fairy tale. With easy stitches and using just tiny amounts of felt you could experiment with different-shaped houses, domed roofs, and decorative details in a range of colors.

Materials

Motif and stitch guide on page 119

2 pieces of felt, 5½ × 2½ in. (14 × 6 cm)

Dressmaker's carbon paper or an air-erasable marker pen

Stranded embroidery floss (cotton) in assorted bright colors

Sewing machine

Matching sewing thread

1 Transfer the design on page 119 onto the center of one of the pieces of felt using dressmaker's carbon paper. If it is difficult to use on the felt, make a template and draw around it with an air-erasable marker and draw in the different sections by eye.

2 Follow the stitch guide on page 119 to embroider the turret, using a selection of bright and contrasting colors.

3 Position the embroidered piece on top of the second piece of felt with wrong sides together, pin, and, leaving a ½-in. (1-cm) border, cut through both pieces around the embroidered shape.

4 Cut a strip of felt 1½ × ½ in. (3.5 × 1 cm). Fold it in half and place the ends between the two pieces of felt at the top, with approx. ½ in. (1 cm) sticking out to form a loop.

5 With wrong sides together, pin the two shapes and machine stitch all around close to the edge, catching the loop in the stitching.

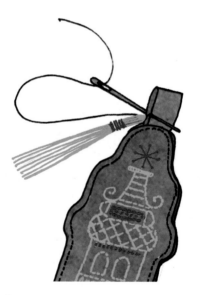

6 Follow the instructions on page 126 to make a tassel from embroidery floss (cotton) and attach it to the loop at the top of the key ring with a few stitches.

Scarf

Based on the traditional embroidery of Eastern Europe and stitched in black on soft woolen fabric, this scarf has a timeless and sophisticated appeal. The fabric I chose in a rich blue-green color has a natural fringe along the selvedge edge. I have left this revealed but fold in a hem if you prefer.

Materials

Motif and stitch guide on page 119

Tracing paper and pencil

Dressmaker's carbon paper

Approx. 55 × 14 in. (140 × 36 cm) soft woolen fabric—you can make your scarf shorter, but I used the whole width of the fabric to include the fringed selvedge

Black stranded embroidery floss (cotton)

1 Enlarge the motif on page 119 by 155 percent and use dressmaker's carbon paper to transfer it onto each end of the fabric. Position the design first in the right-hand corner, 1¼ in. (3 cm) in from the side and bottom edge. Place the tulip facing up. Turn the motif upside down to place the tulip on the opposite end of the scarf.

2 Follow the stitch guide on page 119 to embroider the design in a single color—black makes a strong design element.

3 With right sides facing, fold the length of fabric in half, aligning the raw edges. Pin and machine stitch along the length, taking a ½-in. (1-cm) seam. If you are hemming each end, leave a gap of approx. 2¾ in. (7 cm) in the seam to turn the scarf through.

4 Trim the seam allowance, turn right side out, and press. If you have sewn each end, turn in the raw edges in the gap, and slipstitch the gap closed.

Motifs, stitch guides, and templates

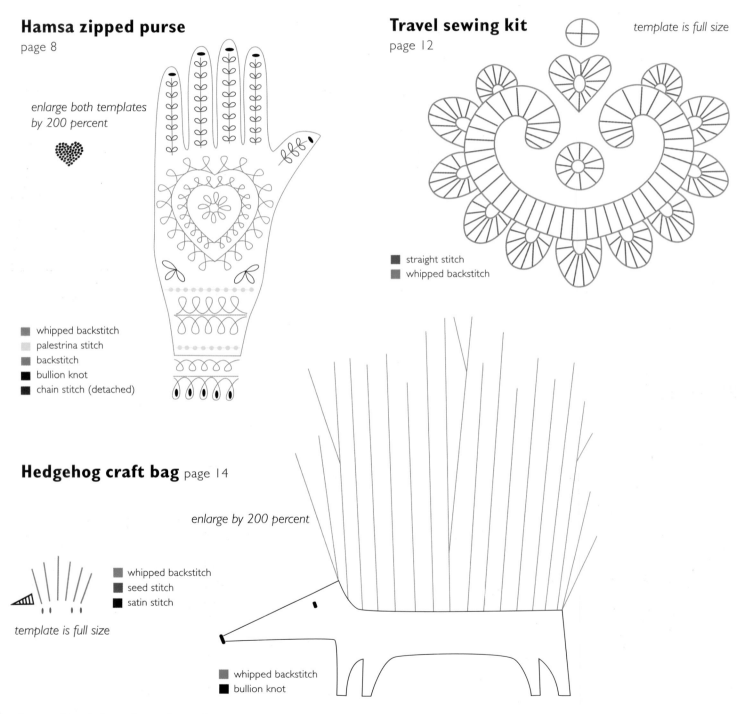

Hamsa zipped purse
page 8

enlarge both templates by 200 percent

■ whipped backstitch
■ palestrina stitch
■ backstitch
■ bullion knot
■ chain stitch (detached)

Travel sewing kit
page 12

template is full size

■ straight stitch
■ whipped backstitch

Hedgehog craft bag page 14

enlarge by 200 percent

■ whipped backstitch
■ seed stitch
■ satin stitch

template is full size

■ whipped backstitch
■ bullion knot

Drawstring bag page 18

enlarge by 155%

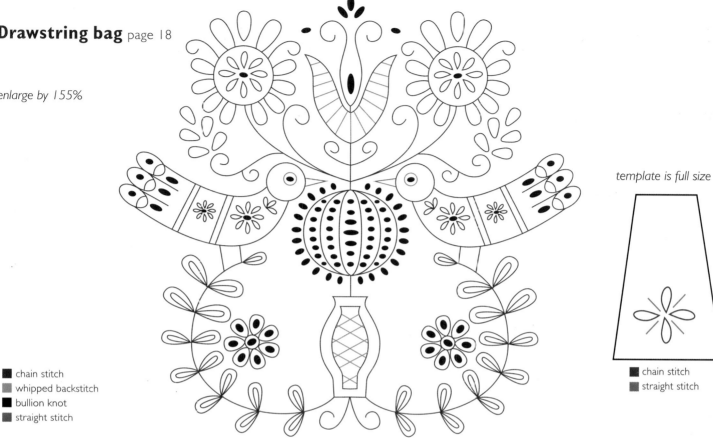

template is full size

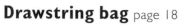

- ▓ chain stitch
- ▓ whipped backstitch
- ■ bullion knot
- ▓ straight stitch

- ▓ chain stitch
- ▓ straight stitch

Picnic bag page 22

enlarge by 155%

- ■ bullion knot

Make-up bag page 27

enlarge by 135%

- ▓ straight stitch
- ▓ backstitch

template is full size

■ whipped backstitch
■ bullion knot
■ straight stitch

Floral booties page 32

enlarge by 135%

cut 4
2 x outer fabric
2 x lining

*Position of embroidery for
the right foot. Place the
embroidery on the other
side for the left foot.*

■ palestrina stitch
■ bullion knot
■ chain stitch

Inca hat page 34

template is full size

■ straight stitch
■ backstitch

Pippi rug page 36

enlarge by 200%

hat template
enlarge by 200%

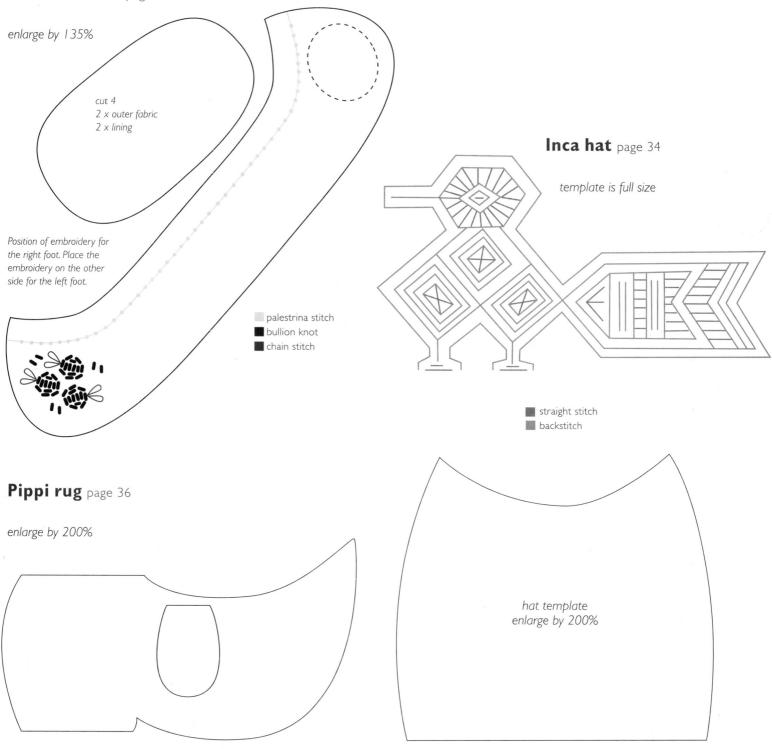

Framed butterfly page 40

enlarge by 155%

■ bullion knot
■ whipped backstitch
■ seed stitch

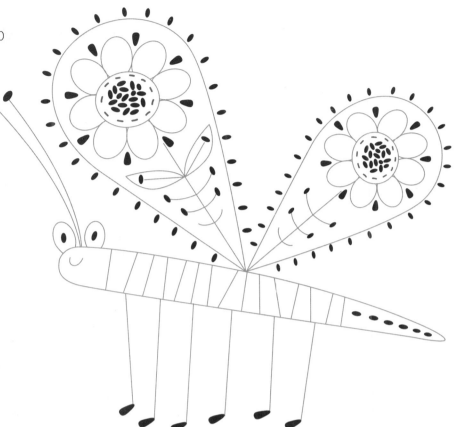

Daisy dress page 43

template is full size

■ cross stitch
■ zigzag stitch
■ bullion knot
■ daisy stitch
■ straight stitch
■ chain stitch (detached)

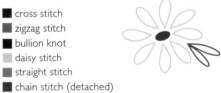

Pin dolls page 46

template is full size

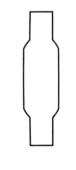

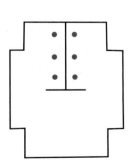

■ straight stitch
■ chain stitch (detached)
■ french knot

Folk doll page 51

enlarge by 200%

■ bullion knot
■ straight stitch

cut 2

cut 4

Appliquéd round pillow
page 55

enlarge template by 135%

■ bullion knot
■ chain stitch (detached)
■ whipped backstitch
■ seed stitch

enlarge by 200%

Indian peacock chair pad page 57

Reindeer pillow page 60

fern stitch
whipped backstitch
seed stitch
chain stitch (detached)
bullion knot
fill area with bullion knots

enlarge by 200%

Sashiko play mat
page 62

enlarge by 135%

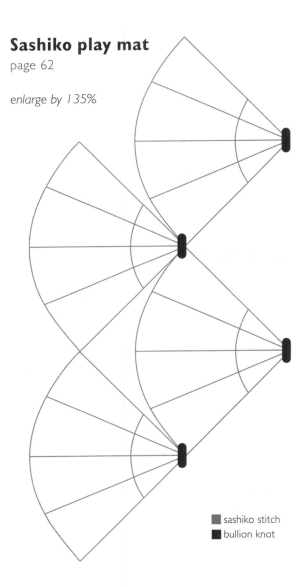

■ sashiko stitch
■ bullion knot

Picnic cloth page 70   *enlarge by 155%*

	1	2	3	4	5	6	7	8	9	10	11	12	13	14	15	16	17	18	19	20	21	22	23	24	25	26
1		●	●	●	●																					
2			●	●	●									✻	✻											
3			□	●	●	●				✻	✻		✻	✻	✻	✻										
4			□	□	●	●	●		✻	X	X	/	✻	✻	✻	O	✻									
5			□	□	□	●	●	✻	X	X	/	/	/	/	X	O	✻									
6				□	□	□	✻	O	✻	/	O	O	✻	✻	✻	/	X	X	✻							
7					□	✻	O	/	X	✻	O	O	O	✻	✻	X	X	O								
8			●	●	●	✻	X	/	X	✻	X	X	O	O	O	✻	/	X	✻							
9			●	●	●	●	X	/	X	✻	/	/	X	O	O	✻	/	X	✻							
10	●		●	●	●	✻	X	/	X	✻	/	/	X	O	✻	✻	/	X	✻							
11		●	●	●	□	✻	O	X	/	X	✻	✻	✻	✻	O	X	X	/	X	✻						
12			□	□	□	✻	O	O	X	/	X	X	O	O	O	X	/	O	O	□						
13						✻	O	X	X	/	X	X	X	X	/	X	●	●	●	□	□	□				
14						✻	O	O	/	/	/	/	/	X	O	✻	●	●	●	□	□					
15							✻	O	O	O	X	X	X	O	✻	✻		●	●	●	□	●		●		
16								✻	✻	□	●	O	O	✻	✻			●	●	●	●	●	●			
17									□	□	●															
18									□	□	●	●														
19									□	□	●	●														
20									●	●																
21									●																	

■ ●
□ □
■ X
■ O
■ /
■ ✻

Tulip seat cover page 72

enlarge by 200%

Spanish fish tablecloth page 74

enlarge by 155%

■ chain stitch
■ bullion knot

■ satin stitch
■ bullion knot
■ whipped backstitch

Little bird letter rack page 76

template is full size

■ straight stitch
■ backstitch
■ chain stitch (detached)
■ palestrina stitch
■ bullion knot

Pot holder page 79

enlarge by 155%

- ■ chain stitch (detached)
- ■ bullion knot
- ■ straight stitch
- ■ backstitch

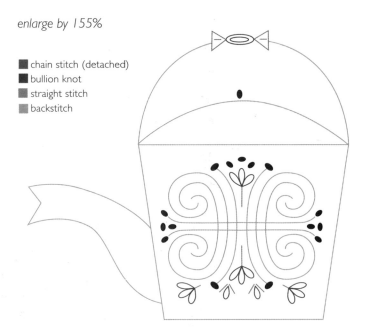

Stripy table mat
page 84

template is full size

- ■ cross stitch
- ■ straight stitch
- ■ zigzag stitch
- ■ fern stitch
- ■ chain stitch (detached)

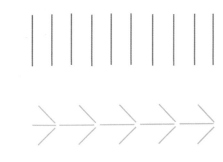

Hanky pocket apron page 87

enlarge by 155%

■ x

Jar cover page 90

template is full size

- ■ bullion knot
- ■ chain stitch (detached)
- ■ straight stitch
- ■ backstitch

Pillowcase page 92

template is full size

- ■ bullion knot
- ■ whipped backstitch

Teacup pincushion page 94

template is full size

- ■ bullion knot
- ■ straight stitch
- ■ backstitch

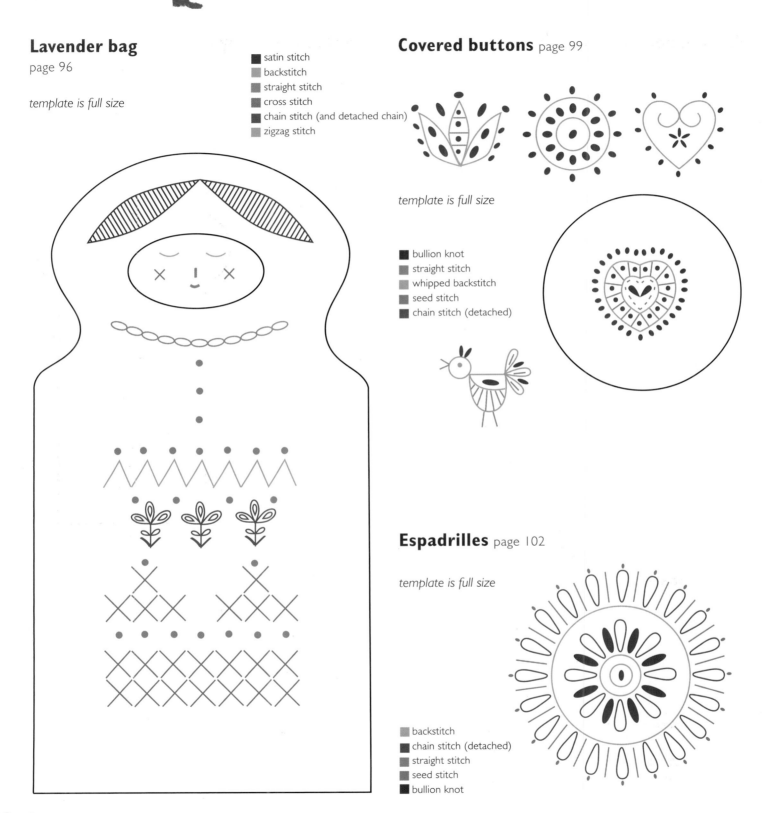

Lavender bag
page 96

template is full size

■ satin stitch
■ backstitch
■ straight stitch
■ cross stitch
■ chain stitch (and detached chain)
■ zigzag stitch

Covered buttons page 99

template is full size

■ bullion knot
■ straight stitch
■ whipped backstitch
■ seed stitch
■ chain stitch (detached)

Espadrilles page 102

template is full size

■ backstitch
■ chain stitch (detached)
■ straight stitch
■ seed stitch
■ bullion knot

Covered notebook page 100

enlarge by 155%

Turreted house key ring page 104

template is full size

- ■ french knot
- ■ whipped backstitch
- ■ backstitch
- ■ straight stitch
- ■ bullion knot
- ■ chain stitch (and detached chain stitch)

- ■ french knot
- ■ backstitch

cut 2

Scarf page 106

enlarge by 155%

- ■ bullion knot
- ■ backstitch

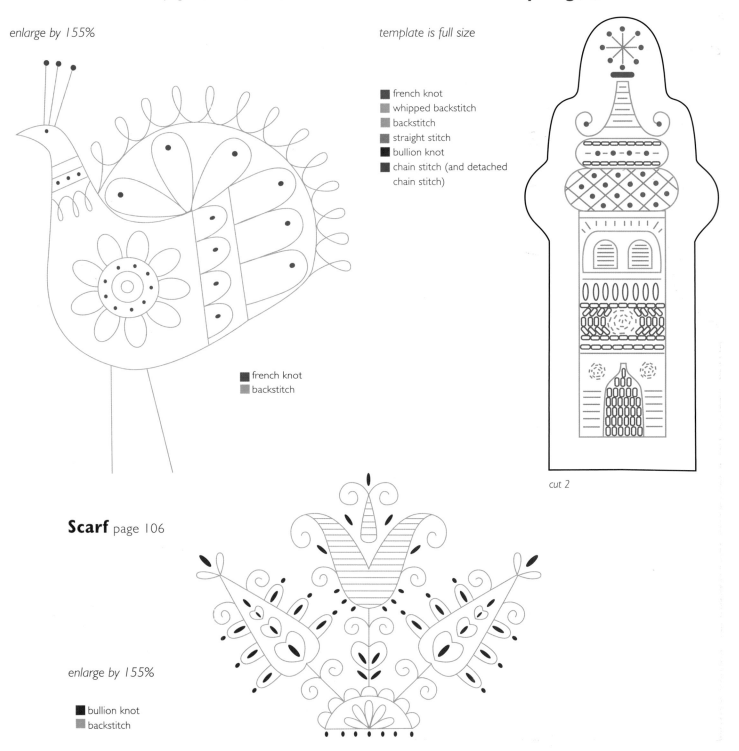

Techniques

tools and equipment

The projects in this book can all be made with very little equipment. A sewing machine is essential, but it can be a very simple model. Even the most basic of modern sewing machines offers a variety of stitches. For this book, you will only need straight stitch and zigzag. But the other stitches that I find very useful on a machine are an automatic one-step button hole, a zigzag overlock-type stitch to neaten raw edges on seams, and a stretch stitch. If you buy a machine with these stitches, then it will also have some decorative stitches such as scallops and hearts, which can be useful.

In addition, you'll need the following:

- Dressmaker's shears for cutting fabric. Never, ever use your dressmaking shears for cutting paper, as this will quickly blunt them.
- Small, sharp-pointed scissors for cutting threads, clipping seam allowances, and trimming.
- Paper scissors for cutting patterns and templates.
- A long ruler, a flexible measuring tape, and a pencil for measuring and marking fabric.
- Tracing paper and a fabric marker pen that either fades away after a couple of days or can be brushed off, and/or dressmaker's carbon paper for transferring motifs to fabric.
- Pins, hand-sewing needles (size 6–8 are a useful medium size), and embroidery needles. The type of embroidery needle depends on the fabric and thread you are using. Sharp-pointed needles called crewels are thin, but are designed to take thicker-than-normal thread and are ideal for most decorative embroidery on plain-weave fabrics. Chenilles are sharp-pointed and heavier, and take thicker threads for work on heavyweight fabrics.
- A steam iron and ironing board are essential for pressing seams.

fabrics and threads

I have used natural fabrics in all the projects, especially linen, cotton, and wool. I also used wool felt for many projects. This can be difficult to source, but you can substitute acrylic felt. Alternatively, try making your own from an old sweater. Make sure that it is 100 percent wool; it won't felt if it contains any man-made fibers. Put the wool items in the washing machine at the hottest setting; they will emerge shrunken, but with that lovely felted look. I sometimes do this twice for a really felted piece.

The other essential is sewing thread. Ideally, try to match the thread type to the fabric (synthetic thread for synthetic fabric, cotton thread for cotton fabric) and match the thread color as closely as possible to the fabric color.

For most of the embroidery projects in this book, I have used stranded embroidery floss (cotton). I usually use all six strands. I have also used pearl cotton and embroidery yarn such as crewel, Persian, or tapestry yarn. However, much depends on the effect you want to create so feel free to experiment.

changing the size of motifs

The project instructions and the templates on pages 108–119 specify how much you need to enlarge motifs in order for your project to be the same size as the ones I made, but you may well wish to adapt a design to make something completely different—so it's worth knowing how to enlarge or reduce motifs to the size you require.

enlarging motifs

First, decide how big you want the pattern or motif to be. Let's say that you want a particular shape to be 10 in. (25 cm) tall.

Then measure the template that you are working from—5 in. (12.5 cm) tall, for example.

Take the size that you want the pattern or motif to be

(10 in./25 cm) and divide it by the actual size of the template (5 in./12.5 cm). Multiply that figure by 100 and you get 200—so you need to enlarge the motif on a photocopier to 200 percent.

If you want to make something that's too big to fit on a standard commercial photocopier, make "registration marks" (either circles or a dotted line) on the original pattern. Enlarge one half of the pattern and then the other, making sure that the registration marks appear on both photocopies, and then tape the two parts of the pattern together, aligning the registration marks.

reducing motifs

If you want a motif on the finished piece to be smaller than the pattern, the process is exactly the same. For example, if the pattern is 5 in. (12.5 cm) tall and you want the motif to be 3 in. (7.5 cm) tall, divide 3 in./7.5 cm by the actual size of the template (5 in./12.5 cm) and multiply by 100, which gives you a figure of 60. So the figure that you need to key in on the photocopier is 60 percent.

transferring patterns and motifs

In most of the projects, you will have to transfer the embroidery pattern or motif onto the fabric. I use three different methods.

The first—and the easiest—is tracing. If the fabric is sheer enough, lay it over the pattern and trace it, using a dressmaker's fade-away marker pen. Alternatively, tape the pattern to a window with the fabric on top, and draw over the lines of the pattern.

The second method is for thick or dark fabrics. Lay dressmaker's carbon paper on the fabric, carbon side down. Lay the embroidery pattern on top and trace over the motif with a ballpoint pen. You can buy carbon paper in different colors suitable for different fabrics.

The final method is for the few fabrics that have a fluffy pile and are difficult to draw on. Trace the motif onto a piece of white tissue paper and pin it onto the fabric. Using cotton sewing thread and a closely spaced running stitch, baste (tack) through the tissue paper and fabric along the pattern lines. Remove the tissue paper, complete the embroidery, and then remove the basting (tacking) stitches.

machine stitching

The key to successful machine stitching is to stitch slowly and in a straight line. Learn to control the speed so that the machine doesn't run away with you!

Straight machine stitch is used for seams; set a stitch length of 10–12 on a scale of 1–20, and a stitch width of 0.

Topstitching is a straight stitch that is stitched from the right side of the fabric. Because it will be visible when the project is completed, it's important to stitch in a straight line. For the projects in this book, topstitching should be done about ⅛ in. (3 mm) from the edge.

Zigzag stitching is used for finishing seam allowances to stop them from fraying and to create a satin-stitch effect in machine embroidery. The stitch width varies depending on the fabric and the desired effect.

basting (tacking)

This is a temporary way of holding two or more pieces of fabric together before stitching, if pins would get in the way. It's useful when making seams in awkward corners, or when sewing curved edges together, or when another layer will be added on top and you wouldn't be able to get at the pins.

To baste (tack) by hand, sew long running stitches (see page 124) and don't secure the thread at the end; when you want to remove the basting (tacking), just snip off the knot at the start of the thread, and pull the other end.

Machine basting is faster than hand basting, and is used to hold a seam or several layers of fabric together temporarily. However, it is not as useful for intricate work as hand basting.

stitching seams

Here is how to stitch the plain seams used in this book.

1 Place two pieces of fabric right sides together, aligning the raw edges. Pin the seam, placing the pins either at right angles to the seamline or along the seamline.

2 If necessary, baste (tack) the seam close to the seamline, just within the seam allowance. With the raw edges on the right, machine stitch a seam of the correct width. To keep the stitching straight, use the stitching guide or a piece of tape the correct distance from the needle.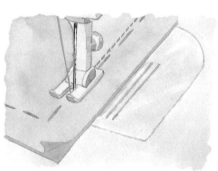

3 At the beginning and end of each seam, do a few stitches in reverse to secure the thread. When stitching around curves, work slowly so that the curve will be continuous and gradual, and you won't stray off the seamline. It helps to use a slightly shorter stitch length here.

4 When you come to a corner, stop ⅝ in. (1.5 cm) from the edge, or whatever the width of the seam is. With the needle at its lowest point, raise the presser foot and pivot the fabric around until the new seamline is in line with the presser foot. Lower the presser foot and continue stitching along the new seamline.

trimming and pressing seams

Seams need to be trimmed and pressed to make them lie flat.

1 On curved seams, clip into the seam allowance after stitching. For inward curves, the clips should be wedge-shaped notches. For outward curves, they just need to be slits.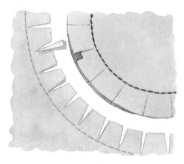

 **2** On a point, trim away the seam allowances around the point. On square corners, snip off the corners of the seam allowances.

3 When a straight piece of fabric is stitched to a corner of another piece, clip into the seam allowance of the straight piece at the corner. This clip will open up and allow the edges to align with the edges  either side of the corner on the other piece. Be careful not to snip beyond the seamline.

 **4** Press seams open from the wrong side, unless instructed otherwise. Do not press seams from the right side, as you may mark the fabric. If stitching together two pieces that already have seams, press open the first seams, snip off the corners of the seam allowances, and align the seams exactly (if appropriate) when pinning the fabric pieces together. While stitching the new seam, keep the seam allowances of the old seams flat.

mitering corners

Mitered corners on a border create a neat, professional-looking finish.

1 Cut each border strip to the desired depth plus the seam allowance; lengthwise, each strip should be the length of the border plus twice the depth of the finished border. Press each border strip in half widthwise, then press the seam allowance along each long raw edge to the wrong side. Open out the strips. With right sides together, aligning the raw edges, pin and baste (tack) the first strip along one edge, leaving the same amount overhanging at each end. Machine stitch along the first crease, leaving the overlap and ½ in. (1 cm) at each end unstitched. Fold back the border strip to the right side, and press.

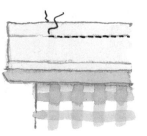

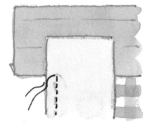

2 Attach the remaining border strips in the same way, taking care not to stitch into the adjoining border strips.

3 Fold each overlapping end of each strip to the wrong side, at a 45° angle. Pin the folds in place from the right side, and slipstitch together, making sure the miters match exactly. Then remove the pins and press the folds.

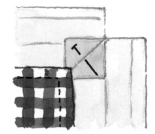

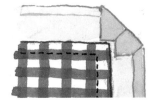

4 Fold in the remaining corners, as shown.

5 Slipstitch along the miter to complete.

hand stitches

There are many embroidery stitches; this section shows the ones I used in the projects, but you can, of course, substitute stitches of your own choice.

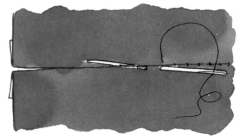

Slipstitch is used to close openings—for example, when you've left a gap in a seam in order to turn a piece right side out—and to appliqué one piece of fabric to another. Work from right to left. Slide the needle between the two pieces of fabric, bringing it out on the edge of the top fabric so that the knot in the thread is hidden between the two layers. Pick up one or two threads from the base fabric, then bring the needle up a short distance along, on the edge of the top fabric, and pull through. Repeat to the end.

Running stitch Work from right to left. Secure the thread with a couple of small stitches, and then make several small stitches by bringing the needle up and back down through the fabric several times along the stitching line. Pull the needle through and repeat. Try to keep the stitches and the spaces between them the same size.

Sashiko stitch This is the same as running stitch except that the space in between each stitch is about a third of the length of the stitch.

Backstitch Work from right to left. Bring the needle up from the back of the fabric, one stitch length to the left of the end of the stitching line. Insert it one stitch length to the right, at the very end of the stitching line, and bring it up again one stitch length in front of the point from which it first emerged. Pull the thread through. To begin the next stitch, insert the needle at the left-hand end of the previous stitch. Continue to the end.

Whipped backstitch Work a line of backstitches (see above). Using a blunt needle, slide the needle under the thread of the first backstitch from top to bottom and pull the thread through. Repeat in each stitch in the row.

Straight stitch can be arranged to form other embroidery stitches, such as seed stitch, star stitch, and zigzag stitch (see above right).

Seed stitch (right) Work pairs of very short straight stitches, positioning them randomly to fill an area.

Star stitch (below) Work a series of straight stitches from the outside of a circle to the center point to create a star shape. If you wish, you can further embellish this stitch by working a French knot at each point of the "star."

Zigzag stitch Work a series of straight stitches in a zigzag formation. This is a useful stitch for decorative borders.

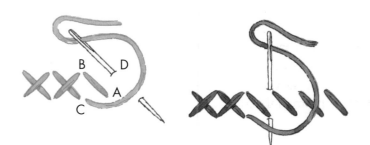

Cross stitch To work a single cross stitch, bring the needle up at A and down at B, then up at C and down at D.

To work a row of cross stitches, work the diagonal stitches in one direction only, from right to left, then reverse the direction and work the second half of the stitch across each stitch made on the first journey.

Herringbone stitch

Bring the needle up at A and down at B to form a diagonal stitch, them come up at C. Go down at D and up at E, ready to start the next stitch.

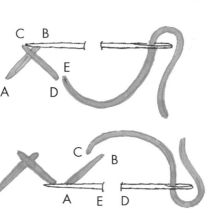

Chain stitch

Bring the needle out at the end of the stitching line. Re-insert it at the same point and bring it out a short distance away, looping the thread around the needle tip. Pull the thread through. To begin the next stitch, insert the needle at the point at which it last emerged, just inside the loop of the previous chain, and bring it out a short distance away, again looping the thread around the needle tip. Repeat to continue.

Detached chain stitch

Work a single chain, as above, but fasten it by taking a small vertical stitch across the bottom of the loop.

Daisy stitch

Work a group of six to eight detached chain stitches in a circle to form a flower shape.

Chain and fly stitch

Work a chain stitch, followed by a fly stitch that forms a v-shape at the base of the chain loop. Tie the stitch down by working a small vertical stitch across the base of the v-shape. This stitch can be worked singly or in rows.

French knot

Bring the needle up from the back of the fabric to the front. Wrap the thread two or three times around the tip of the needle, then reinsert the needle at the point where it first emerged, holding the wrapped threads with the thumbnail of your non-stitching hand, and pull the needle all the way through. The wraps will form a knot on the surface of the fabric.

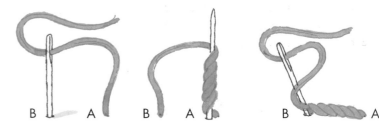

Bullion knot

This is similar to a French knot, but creates a longer coil of thread rather than a single knot. Bring the needle up at A and take it down at B, leaving a loose loop of thread—the distance from A to B being the length of knot that you require. Bring the needle back up at A and wrap the thread around the needle five to eight times, depending on how long you want the knot to be. Hold the wrapped thread in place with your left hand and pull the needle all the way through. Insert the needle at B and pull through, easing the coiled stitches neatly into position. Check each template to see what size bullion knot is required for each project.

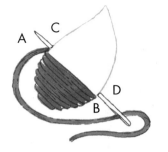

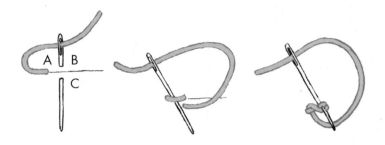

Satin stitch This is a "filling" stitch that is useful for motifs such as flower petals and leaves. Work from left to right. Draw the shape on the fabric, then work straight stitches across it, coming up at A and down at B, then up at C and down at D, and so on. Place the stitches next to each other, so that no fabric can be seen between them. You can also work a row of backstitch around the edge to define the outline more clearly.

Palestrina stitch Bring the needle to the front of the fabric at A. Put the needle in above the line at B and bring it out below the line at C. Take the needle under the stitch from the top to the bottom without catching the fabric. Pull through gently. Bring the needle around and take it under the same stitch, to the right of the last pass and keeping the thread below the needle. Pull the thread through gently. Continue as required.

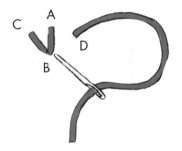

Fern stitch Bring the needle to the front of the fabric at A and put it in at B. Bring the needle out at C and put it in at B. Then bring it out again at D and again put it in at B to complete the stitch. Bring the needle out just below B to continue.

embellishments

Making tassels To make a tassel, wind some embroidery floss (cotton) around three fingers a few times. Slip the floss from your fingers and wind a length of floss around one end. Tie with a knot to secure. Trim the loops at the opposite end to make a tassel approx. 1½ in. (3.5 cm) long.